THE
CARRIAGE
AND
WAGON
WORKS

OF THE
GWR AT
SWINDON

SWINDON RAILWAY WORKS IN THE GREAT WESTERN STEAM YEARS

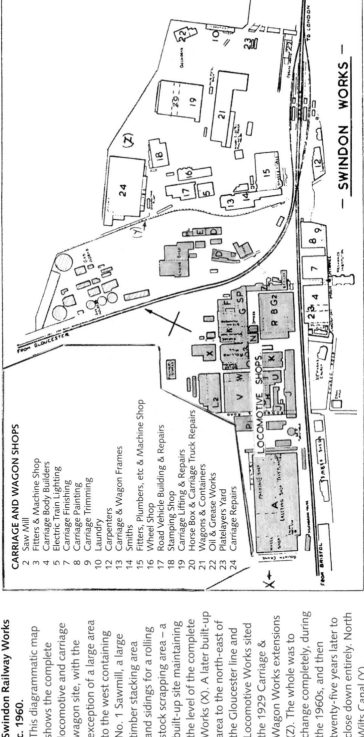

CARRIAGE AND WAGON SHOPS

2 Saw Mill
3 Fitters & Machine Shop
4 Carriage Body Builders
5 Electric Train Lighting
7 Carriage Finishing
8 Carriage Painting
9 Carriage Trimming
10 Laundry
12 Carpenters
13 Carriage & Wagon Frames
14 Smiths
15 Fitters, Plumbers, etc & Machine Shop
16 Wheel Shop
17 Road Vehicle Building & Repairs
18 Stamping Shop
19 Carriage Lifting & Repairs
20 Horse Box & Carriage Truck Repairs
21 Wagons & Containers
22 Oil & Grease Works
23 Platelayers Yard
24 Carriage Repairs

Swindon Railway Works c. 1960.

This diagrammatic map shows the complete locomotive and carriage wagon site, with the exception of a large area to the west containing No. 1 Sawmill, a large timber stacking area and sidings for a rolling stock scrapping area – a built-up site maintaining the level of the complete Works (X). A later built-up area to the north-east of the Gloucester line and Locomotive Works sited the 1929 Carriage & Wagon Works extensions (Z). The whole was to change completely, during the 1960s, and then twenty-five years later to close down entirely. North Wilts Canal (Y).

THE CARRIAGE AND WAGON WORKS OF THE GWR AT SWINDON

KEN GIBBS

The
History
Press

Cover illustrations: front, top: No. 9 Trimming Shop; bottom: bogie assembly in No. 19 Carriage Lifting Shop; back: No. 15 Fitting and Machining Shop. (All author's collection)

First published 2016

The History Press
The Mill, Brimscombe Port
Stroud, Gloucestershire, GL5 2QG
www.thehistorypress.co.uk

British Library Cataloguing in Publication Data.
A catalogue record for this book is available from the British Library.

ISBN 978 0 7509 6419 7

Typesetting and origination by The History Press

Printed and bound in Great Britain by TJ International Ltd.

CONTENTS

1

THE CARRIAGE & WAGON WORKS AT SWINDON

INTRODUCTION

The Great Western Railway Works at Swindon was known and is remembered, as are its trained craftsmen, all over the railways of the world. It has been written about, discussed, filmed, and lectured on countless times. Many of its old steam locomotives saved from the scrap yards and lovingly rebuilt, often by amateurs, are still being written about, discussed, and can be seen in action once again, running on heritage lines. These have been described and illustrated, in literally hundreds of books, ever since the steam locomotive's birth in 1804. In all of this activity, only a half of the Swindon Works site is fleetingly 'mentioned in passing' and is only occasionally represented in illustrations. There is usually very little descriptive matter about the 'other half' of the successful operation of a railway works system, the design, construction and repair of the rolling stock, or the carriages and wagons. Where it was done is often mentioned, the finished item illustrated many times, but not *how* they did it! A railway system which began with a variety of tram roads and plateways, where little wagons full of stone and coal traversed comparatively short distances from mine or quarry to the nearest canal were pulled by horse power over rails of materials varying from wood strips to iron rails, developed into a passenger-carrying, fast, comfortable and safe transport system all over the world.

The introduction of mobile steam power by Trevithick in 1804, transformed the entrepreneurial world of transport into a new and profitable age of development; the transport revolution had begun.

Alongside those developments that eventually replaced the horse, although it didn't happen immediately, the thoughts of something better than a little four-wheeled wagon which had transported stone and coal was required for the transport of members of the public – those daring enough, in the early days of rail, to risk their lives behind a coal- or coke-fired iron monster which breathed out smoke and steam.

Opening of the Stockton and Darlington Line
'Locomotive No. 1 (driven by George Stephenson); six wagons loaded with coal and flour; a covered coach for directors and proprietors; twenty-one coal wagons fitted for passengers (450 of them!); six more wagons loaded with coals.' Stephenson reputedly told the man with the flag to 'clear off' as he wanted to 'get moving!' which he did at 15mph! (Illustration and data from *Our Iron Roads* 1883 by F.S. Williams)

Even at this early stage, the 'class distinction' of the period raised its head, continuing for a number of years, as evidenced by the inaugural run of the first official opening of a passenger transport system, the Stephenson-inspired Stockton and Darlington Railway opening on 27 September 1825 (as commemorated in the above illustration).

The development of passenger traffic was well under way and was followed a decade later by the Great Western Railway (GWR). The GWR's locomotive development has been extensively covered elsewhere but the growth and development of its carriage and wagon construction, symbolised by the new workshops at Swindon in 1843, has been relatively overlooked. Until now, that is.

SOME DEVELOPMENT PROBLEMS AT SWINDON

Up to the 1870s the extent of the Works to the west ended at the Rodbourne Lane (later 'road'), which crossed the main London–Bristol railway line by means of a level crossing. As the years and development rolled on, an extensive area of land was selected for development to the west of Rodbourne Lane, and the level crossing disappeared under what developed as an extensive bridge system with a lowered road which now passed underneath the bridges – the road being lowered to cope with the introduction of the double-decker bus.

Bridges over sunken roads, like the Whitehouse Bridges, often cause problems, and another one of the roads under the centre of the Works area, although on the flat, certainly does. With increasing frequency, lorries get stuck by running into the bridge and jamming themselves underneath it. With so many warning and height restriction signs it's baffling why the problem still occurs!

The western development of the Works supported an embankment carrying the line out of Swindon Works and onto the West and Bristol. The embankment already passed over the River Ray and onto a bridge over the Wootton Bassett road, which, along with the embankment of the Midland South Western Junction railway, formed an extremity boundary of a section of the railway land. Incidentally, this is also yet another bridge under which lorries regularly get stuck. Any expansion of this area would also entail dealing with the River Ray and with the land and filling already well advanced by 1900, completion and 'settling' was finished, as shown on the following map from 1920.

Something which those who live in Swindon probably do not realise is that the Works is on a much higher level than the rest of the new town, which in itself came into being because of the Railway Works. This was presumably because it was initially built on a natural flat area of suitable size, a flat small hill. The old town or village of Swindon as it stood, was on a considerable hill above the proposed Works site and a couple of miles away.

As the Works developed, the height differences with the surrounding ground became a problem. Again, those who live in Swindon may not realise that all railway lines emanating through or from the Works leave Swindon both to east and west on quite high embankments. Thus for expansion, much of the ground had to be built-up and 'thereby hangs a tale' as the saying has it. (Any hill or raised ground on the proposed route of the railway was levelled, where convenient, or if a hill, then by a 'cutting', the excavated soil put to good use – a good example being the Salford and Tiverton cutting for the estimated 583,440 cubic yards of spoil required for the Salford Embankment.)

Any expansion of the original layout to the west of the Works required tons of filler material, where tipping was to continue for a number of years. The usual 'cutting' material was augmented by train loads of waste from the Welsh mines and quarries to make up the area eventually covering No. 1 Sawmill – the area for timber, drying and stacking, the kiln drying building and the locomotive scrapping area, all of which were to be developed later when the ground had settled. This area, however, had one small problem – a little river called the Ray. To avoid the hassle of a large diversion, a brickwork tunnel was constructed over the dumping area thereby surmounting the small but bothersome river.

Filler dumping proceeded for a number of years until a prominent area was formed, about 20ft high at the western extremity. (Later filling occurred to the north east of the site for further expansion of the Carriage & Wagon Works.)

Having consolidated, a major problem arose during the Second World War for the GWR. The waste dumped from the Welsh collieries, called 'slack', contained an amount of inflammable material, coal fragments and dust etc., and in the early 1930s smoke was observed coming from cracks in the ground. Various borings were made, and a red-hot area of spontaneous combustion was later found deep

Making a 'cutting' and an embankment, *c.*1880: having reached the bottom level of the cutting, a line of railway wagons can take away the spoil, all removed by hand. The artist has made it look like a mountainside! (*Our Iron Roads*, 1883)

A tough job: getting to the bottom before a rail track could be laid, without any power assistance, entailed hard manual labour assisted by the plodding horse with a rope attached and running over a pulley arrangement to assist the diggers to guide the spoil barrows up the sides of the cutting.

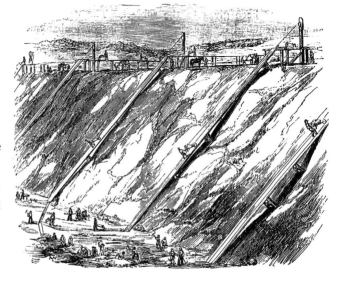

Building an embankment by horse and wagon – a lengthy process!

down in the embankment. Gallons of water were poured in. The burning mass was discovered to be approaching the brickwork tunnel over the river. Various areas of spoil were collapsing and the flames were now visible at night, which became an added source of anxiety, as the company feared the flames might provide a beacon for German bombers. Digging out continued and a large trench was excavated, which stopped the flare reaching the brickwork, and the area of timber staked with air spaces to assist with the drying out process!

Much of the embankment at the end of Swindon Works as a going concern was used again for filling, this time for the motorway construction! This filling caused several other problems. In the Loco Works Stamping Shop, the built-up area of the floor level caused the drop hammer frames, positioned sideways to the west, to begin to tilt due to the shaking caused by the blow when the free-fall 'hammer' or 'tup' dropped. The biggest new hammer, therefore, was placed crossways north to south to avoid the tilting, which seemed to work! (It's lower hammer block is a 68-ton casting made at the Works and is still in position, but buried.)

A further problem occurred at the Foundry. Big castings, too big for the usual separate 'moulding box' were cast actually in the earth floor; the sand mould was thus below floor level. On one occasion, when the metal was poured for a bronze pump-barrel casting it broke through the sand mould, the earth having collapsed under it, and the molten metal solidified as a giant bronze spider in the cracks and holes under the casting area, reputedly about 6 tons in weight, and had to be dug out by hand!

All casting was done in the Locomotive section of the Works as the Carriage and Wagon (C&W) section, although it developed, had no foundry. The development of the Works, including the different C&W Workshops, are listed as follows:

SWINDON CARRIAGE & WAGON WORKS

No. 1	Shop Sawmill (West End)
No. 2	Sawmill
No. 3	Fitting and Machining
No. 4	Carriage Body Building and Repairs
No. 5	Train Lighting Equipment (Electrical) includes Battery Repair
No. 6	Carriage Body Repairs
No. 7	Carriage Finishing – Interior Woodwork, Doors and Panels
No. 8	Carriage Painting
No. 9	Carriage Trimming – Seat Covers etc.
No. 9a	Lining Sewers (Female) – Part of Trimming Function
No. 10	Laundry (Female)
No. 10a	Polishers (Female) – French Polishing
No. 11	General Labourers
No. 12	Carpenters
No. 12a	Polishers – French Polishers
No. 13	Wagon Frame Building
No. 13a	Carriage Frame Repairs
No. 14	Blacksmiths
No. 15	Fitting, Turning and Machinists
No. 15a	Gas and Steam Fitters, Plumbers, Copper and Tin Smiths
No. 16	Wheel Repairs
No. 16a	Case Hardening and Heat Treatment
No. 17	Road Vehicle Building and Repair – Carts, Trailers etc.
No. 18	Stamping Shop
No. 19	Shop Complex
No. 19a	Carriage Trimmers – Repairs
No. 19b	Carriage Finishers – Repairs
No. 19c	Carriage Lifters
No. 19d	Vacuum Brake and Carriage Bogie Repairs
No. 20	Horsebox and Carriage Truck Repairs
No. 21	Wagon Building and Repairs – Wood
No. 21a	Wagon Repairs – Iron
No. 21b	Wagon Painting
No. 22	Oil and Grease Works
No. 23	Platelayers' Yard, Maintenance and Breakers
No. 24	Carriage Paint Repairs
No. 24a	Carriage Body Repairs – an area of over 7 acres

Richard (handwritten, beside No. 3)
Richard (handwritten, beside No. 16)

SWINDON CARRIAGE & WAGON WORKS MANAGEMENT

1837–1864	Daniel Gooch	Locomotive Superintendent
1864–1877	Joseph Armstrong	Locomotive Carriage & Wagon Superintendent
1877–1902	William Dean	Locomotive Carriage & Wagon Superintendent
1902–1921	George Churchward	CM&EE & Locomotive Carriage & Wagon Superintendent
1922–1941	C.B. Collett	Chief Mechanical Engineer
1941–1949	Frederick Hawksworth	Chief Mechanical Engineer
1950–1951	H. Randall	Carriage & Wagon Engineer
1951–1956	C.A. Roberts	Carriage & Wagon Engineer
1956–1962	R.A. Smeddle	Chief Mechanical Engineer

CARRIAGE & WAGON WORKS MANAGERS

1868–1873	T.G. Clayton	Design of the C&W Workshops at Swindon
1873–1885	J. Holden	
1885–1895	G. Churchward	
1895–1901	L.R. Thomas	
1901–1902	T.O. Hogarth	
1902–1920	F.W. Marillier	Coped with the First World War years
1920–1922	C.C. Champeney	
1922–	R.G. Hannington	
1922–1946	E.T. Evans	
1946–1947	H. Randle	
1947–1948	C.T. Roberts	
1948–1962	H.G. Johnson	
(1962–1967)	J.S. Scott	Chief Works Manager
1962–1963	E.T. Butcher	

WORKS MANAGERS – LOCO, CARRIAGE & WAGON WORKS COMBINED

1967–1972	H.W. Mear
1972–1981	H.R. Roberts
1981–1987	H. Taylor

1987–Present Combined Locomotive Works and Carriage & Wagon Works now closed

The areas originally covered by the Locomotive Works and the Carriage & Wagon Works were split approximately 50:50 between the two, over a total of 280 acres. On complete closure of the Carriage & Wagon Works area, much of the work was lost to other rail workshops, and the remaining C&W work transferred to the now empty shops in the Locomotive section of the Works. The C&W area now sold off for further development. The Locomotive Works area is now a housing development, shopping centre and a museum of the Great Western Railway (utilising those buildings still standing). The original site covered an area of 1.5 miles x 0.33 miles.

2

ITS LIFE AND TIMES

The birth of the Great Western Railway has been well documented. The work of Brunel and Gooch in establishing a railway to join London to Bristol, seemingly in the early stages at least, ignoring anything else to north or south, was initially conditioned by one major factor. Contrary to the beliefs of a certain group of people, the earth is not flat, particularly the fraction of it selected for the track of the proposed railway.

The flat bits had already been commandeered by other transport systems in addition to the ribbon of the Great West Road. The Wilts & Berks Canal had already grabbed the best route and the meandering, wandering course of the Thames & Severn Canal got in the way of any future development. The two canals were linked by the North Wilts Canal, which eventually split the Works site. A route to the north of the Wilts & Berks Canal was thus the only viable alternative, but even the most desirable sections still contained high spots and depressions, all to be included in whatever way was considered best by Brunel's surveying efforts. Whilst the canals had cuttings through hills, or 'locks' to raise and lower the boats to the route level; the latter system was of no use for a railway! It was decided quite early on that the comparatively flatter section selected for the route from London as far as the Vale of the White Horse, near the little town-on-the-hill of Swindon, could be covered by trains reasonably speedily. From Swindon to the west, however, a change of locomotive would be required. So … it was Swindon that provided a suitable place for a maintenance depot, where locomotives could be changed to a design which could most easily cope with hilly sections toward Bristol.

A precise spot was chosen in the Vale – at the joint in the London–Bristol track where construction of a branch of a separate railway already under way (soon to be owned by Great Western) forked off toward Cheltenham and Gloucester – and the idea of Swindon Works was born. The land in question had been purchased by the Cheltenham Railway Company from two vendors, the first a Mr Sheppard and then Mr Villett, both of Swindon. The company was rather pressed for finance to aid any growth or expansion and so part of the deal was that the land should be developed for a repair facility and station, which fell right into the Great Western's lap – the Great Western having purchased a second smaller section from Mr Villett.

After several presentations to parliament by Brunel, and several rejections, the proposal originally for the launch of the 'London and Bristol Rail Road' was resubmitted with new figures and was eventually passed as the 'Great Western Railway'!

Brunel had difficulty in establishing accurate earth-working costs; initially estimated at one shilling per cubic yard, these were found to be much higher at 19 pence. The estimates had proven to be too low! In this case, the initial £2.8 million estimated cost ended up being more like £6.25 million! However, with everything settled, the Great Western Works design could go ahead.

Looking at the 1846 map of the Works layout, it shows the workshops of the usual locomotive engineering requirements, with only one shop specifically for 'wagons', with no mention of carriages, although they certainly existed and were produced by a range of private road-carriage manufacturers, detailed later. The woodworking craftsmanship employed in the manufacture of the road carriages, in which these private manufacturers had much experience, was carried over into the designs for the first railway carriages, as shown in the following illustration.

The 1840s and 1850s saw the battles of the 'gauge war' where contenders appeared to be forever obtaining acts for one gauge or the other, with running powers over adjacent lines. Having settled for one gauge, along comes an act for installing the other. Some wished to remove the broad-gauge rails with which they had started but were forbidden to do so by the 1846 Act. One company, the Midland, sold off its broad-gauge stock but were still stuck with some of the broad-gauge track covered by the act – one colliery line until 1882.

Various rights afforded to the Avon & Gloucestershire Railway, and preserved in the 1839 Act, allowed narrow-gauge rails to be laid inside the broad track. Although only about 2.5 miles long, it became the first mixed track in the country. And so it went on, the 'break of gauge' still a major stumbling block, and the opposition continued to grow.

In June 1845, a commission had been set up to discuss the problem and a trial of locomotive power, safety, speed and comfort compared. Whilst the broad gauge won hands down, the inconvenience of the two gauges was the governing factor in the decision, which concluded with the following:

That the gauge of 4ft 8½ inches be declared by the legislature to be the gauge used in all public railways now under construction or hereafter to be constructed in Great Britain.

That, unless by consent of the legislature, it should not be permitted to the directors of any railway company to alter the gauge of such a railway.

It continued with examination of how adaptations could be made for use of vehicles to use either gauge, by using wheels sliding on broad gauge axles etc ...

Criticism was followed by:

> Adverting to the vast expense which must be involved in an entire alteration of the broad gauge, and having regard to the circumstances under which the companies employing this gauge were established and to the interests they have acquired, my Lords do not feel themselves justified in recommending that it should be proposed to Parliament to compel the entire reduction of the seven feet gauge ... cannot sanction such an expense ... Companies to which the broad gauge railways belong, cannot be called upon to incur such an expense themselves ... therefore we are unable to suggest any other equitable or practical means by which the desired uniformity of gauge could be obtained.
>
> Any lines south of a line London to Bristol for which Acts have already been obtained should be permitted to be constructed, as originally intended.

So, checkmate or a typical fudge! The broad gauge staggered on, whilst the narrow gauge opposition continued to flourish, made stronger by the succession of Amalgamation Acts that tied several of such narrow-gauge companies together.

The Great Western became involved in a downturn in investment and the enforcing, by law, of the financing of various branch lines. To complicate matters, Daniel Gooch, one of the 'founder fathers' of the company, around the end of the 1850s was becoming more and more disillusioned with the board members; various directors appointed had certainly not really been his choice and, as result, relationships were becoming rather strained. All of this, coupled with the death of Brunel in 1859, led to a new era in the structure of the Great Western for the approaching new decade of the 1860s.

The 1860s brought a period of turmoil to the progress of the Great Western Railway. In tandem with the development of the Great Western Railway was the increasing worry over the spread of other railway companies introducing the narrow, 4ft 8½in gauge lines. This was also a period of financial problems for the Great Western. Gooch had increasing health problems and was advised to take a holiday and on his return had an urgent message regarding the railway problems. He once again clashed with the board and, desiring a change, joined the company about to attempt the laying of the Atlantic cable by the steamship *Great Eastern*, of which he was part owner, resigning from the Great Western in 1864.

After arguments about his successor, he was pleased when Armstrong of Wolverhampton Works was appointed to follow him in 1864 as the Locomotive, C&W superintendent. The C&W superintendent had previously been J. Gibson (of the famous 'Gibson Ring' for locking tyres on railway wheels), and the position had now been added to that of the newly appointed Armstrong, whose headquarters would now be Swindon.

The year after his appointment a very controversial proposal was made. The Great Western had only the Carriage Maintenance Shops at Paddington, all new carriages were supplied by outside private firms. The repair function had been also undertaken at Saltney Works (Chester), Coleham, Shrewsbury and Worcester Works, the latter being burned down by a disastrous fire in 1864 when eighteen new carriages were destroyed. The proposal centred on a C&W Works at Oxford, selected by some 'experts' as 'being ideal', but on examination of the site it was found to be a flood plain often overrun by the Thames! (An area with inherent problems to be faced in later years!)

A petition forwarded by the notables of business interests in Swindon (further boosted by requests and pressure from officers and staff at Swindon) was submitted, requesting that a carriage works be added to the wagon building at the site of the existing Locomotive Works at Swindon. The petition, as well as the strong objections from the academics at the university town who had no wish for the academia to have to possibly mix with the 'blue collar and labouring classes' of the C&W environs, put Swindon well to the top of the list of possible sites. Didcot was also on the list but it was recorded that 'Didcot is a wilderness where craftsmen cannot live!' Not a good recommendation, which must have rather annoyed the residents.

Gooch was now away from the railway for a time. Among his activities on the *Great Eastern*, which involved an unsuccessful cable-laying venture when the cable broke well out into the Atlantic and his return to shore, he had also won a parliamentary seat. He was very surprised on return to find Mr Potter, the chairman, had resigned having amassed a large expansion based debt and was pressed from all sides to take on the job and save the company from a growing potential of bankruptcy. He immediately stopped some of the schemes initiated by Potter, those that is, which had not progressed too far, and removed the tentative agreements relating to the new Carriage Works being sited at Oxford.

Having settled the immediate problems, it was back aboard the *Great Eastern* and to have another go at salvaging the abortive first attempt at cable laying by tracking the broken ends, splicing in a new piece with a second cable proceeding to Newfoundland. For this, he was awarded a baronetcy by Queen Victoria. The euphoria was to be short lived however, returning to find the situation back to square one with the collapse of several banks and other railway companies which had entrusted their finances to them.

Approaching the government for a possible loan, the chancellor (who at that time was Disraeli) refused to assist, but by very tight budgeting, including reducing the number of directors from twenty-six to sixteen, the Great Western scraped by out of the mess. By 1867 the crisis had all but passed but there were still some drastic cuts to be made, and, as usual, the first thing to suffer were the maintenance frequencies of the locos and rolling stock, leading passengers to record increasingly objections to the condition of some rolling stock.

The proposed cost of carriage works at Oxford had been estimated at about £80,000 but this was re-estimated, analysing potential requirements of 100 carriages and fifty wagons, first estimated at £26,000, but reviewed and minuted at £21,000.

There were also proposals at this time for additional locomotives which would take much longer planning time for development, the C&W requirements a more urgent priority. Two men were selected for this planning job, William Dean and Thomas Clayton. Both completely different characters – Dean a locomotive man to the core, both practical and academic, whilst Clayton originally trained as a pattern maker – were to aggressively follow, to the letter, Armstrong's vision for his new C&W Works.

By the end of 1868, the first C&W building (420ft x 265ft) was completed south of the mainline on land already owned by the Great Western, an act which constituted a massive cost saving with potential for the rest of the large expanse to be developed, a part of which would form the Great Western housing estate.

The increasing importance of the embryo Swindon Railway Works was not lost to the owners of any land adjacent to the site, and the 1880s saw land purchased from local worthies increasing in value per acre with every breath drawn in the vital negotiations! These negotiations had added several parcels of land, each of about 20 acres, but that the cost to expand the Locomotive Works was higher per acre than that designated for the C&W Works.

On the following 1890 map, the large Wagon Lifting Shop (later No. 21 Shop) can be seen, adjacent to the surviving farm buildings on the purchased land. The expansion was of great importance due to the 1892 demise of broad gauge and the required storage for locomotives, carriages and wagons for conversion and/or scrapping, which continued apace.

One innovation of 1903 was the introduction of the steam rail motor, a 60ft and then a 70ft carriage with a steam-powered bogie at one end. These are really a story by themselves.[1] This innovation ultimately proved too successful; the traffic these rural vehicles produced was such that they could not cope and were rapidly replaced (delayed by the First World War) over a period of twenty or so years by the push–pull small locomotive and a trailer carriage – often plus the wagons which the steam rail motors could not handle. Events leading up to the twentieth century had emphasised the fact that an extensive stock increase of locos, carriages

---

1. See my book *The Steam Rail Motors of the Great Western Railway* (Stroud: The History Press, 2015).

and wagons would also require the premises in which to construct and maintain them. New finance legislation following in 1911 meant a strict official scrutiny of costs, and the instigation of a special investigation. This resulted in three reports for the three categories of construction, for locomotives, carriages and wagons.

The locomotive section was first tackled with very detailed and extensive further plans, but examining the 1900 Works Plan on page 30 shows that during the 1890s extensive work had already considerably expanded the C&W Works with a further Carriage Lifting Shop and a Carriage Stock Shed. Also, additional to that in the Locomotive Works, the C&W Works had its own 'Stamping' Shop (No. 18 Shop). From the word go, the Works had had a problem with the water supply, and it will be seen from the layout plans for the years up to 1900 there were two reservoirs (later consolidated into one) covering a large area of the C&W site. Improvements in supply enabled the reservoirs to be filled in. This, although essential for use of the site, left the builders of the extensions to the Carriage Brake Shop with a major problem and, to obtain firm foundations, excavations had to go down nearly 30ft with the brickwork for one corner of the new shop, which became the No. 15 C&W Machine and Fitting Shop.

The Great Western, noted for 'making everything', had also made its own bricks, and a Loco Works engine shed extension in 1907 utilised the brickmaking site. Stockpiled clay was used to fill part of the reservoir. Whilst this was occurring at the eastern end of the C&W site, a development was under way at the site's western extremity on the area of the built-up embankment which included a timber shed and a sawmill section to deal with the trunks for logging, transferred from the existing mill on the centre section of the Works site. This allowed the mill from which it had been removed to then concentrate on the preparation of the cut wood into the sections required for the vehicle construction programmes and maintenance within the Works, becoming No. 1 & 2 Shops.

In the middle of what can only be called a depression, the problem was made worse by a disastrous loss of stock in a major fire in the Carriage Paint Shop (an accident?) in the middle of a lay-off of staff followed by a railway strike call for 18 August 1911. Not affecting the Swindon Works as such, it did contribute to the amalgamation of several unions into the formation of the National Union of Railwaymen (NUR). This was also the period of strict financial scrutiny mentioned earlier so, although expansion plans were formulated, a major investigation into the proposals was instigated, resulting in a restriction to locomotive expansion only.

Whilst work on the locomotive side progressed very slowly from the delayed reports of the investigation, in 1915 an analysis of carriage life was determined at thirty-three years and a wagon analysis followed the same lines. Carriage & Wagon side building extensions to the Carriage Stock Washing and Lifting Sheds, a new laundry and a quite extensive addition to the Wagon Shop were shelved, occurring 'as-and-when' over the next two decades, as finance would be allocated, and the effects of the 1914–18 war were dealt with.

The First World War put great pressure on requirements and an extensive carriage building programme already in existence was absorbed into war requirements for furnishing ambulance trains. With wagons, specialist vehicles were built or existing vehicles modified, for example horse-drawn transport and specialist road wagons. Even the Trimming Shop was involved with special webbing, carrying bags, saddlery etc. A total of 216,350 wagons, 'goods' and bogie types were the war period contribution.

The technical advance in certain materials shows that, comparing the 1910 plan of the C&W Works with that produced in 1920, only one real addition building-wise was made in the period. This was the new Oil Works, now a separate building, with the existing Grease Works retained.

The exigencies of the war caused disruption for the Works, as war production had taken over areas of some workshops, particularly in the locomotive shops, for work which was completely alien to the steam locomotive – large guns and carriages, shells, bombs and other components, which interrupted the maintenance function of the rolling stock. The C&W requirements were in general in line with what was normally done in the workshops, although certain different fittings were required – the ambulance trains and alterations to some wagon designs, for example, were outside the normal run of work. At the end of the war, the returning workforce from the services were now expecting to return to the jobs they had been doing, in a number of cases now undertaken by females, so problems of staffing complicated the return to normal working practices.

Reorganisation was now the order of the day, and, short of actual 'nationalisation' of the railways, the formation of the 'Big Four' (GWR, LMS, LNER, SR) caused a further approach to organisational chaos for several years from 1921.

With the Great Western Railway, any thing or company, either profitable or potential rival, had long ago been absorbed or put out of business as the Great Western expanded. Those companies now absorbed were added to the host of GWR problems with their 'non-standard' mix of private-company made rolling stock, which was eventually either scrapped as 'not acceptable' or 'Great Westernised' where possible.

The coming decade, the 1920s, was one of boom and bust economy, lay-offs of staff, strikes over pay and conditions, and a general shortage of work. This was not the case, however, in the C&W, where building work, although slow to begin with, progressed considerably. It was during this period that the Locomotive Works extensions were finally completed. The production rates improved continuously, that is, until the whole period ground to a halt with the disastrous General Strike of 1926 bringing about, or continuing, the short-time working and lower wages for staff into the next decade and further problems! One possible brighter highlight of the previous decade had been the fleeting visit in 1924 of King George and Queen Mary, visiting the C&W Works Sawmill, Carriage Body Building No. 4 Shop, Trimming, Finishing and French Polishing Shops and the Locomotive Works. The effect of the General Strike, whilst lasting and affecting the railways for a period of only seven to ten days, really hit the Great Western Railway in a different way with a lasting drop in the once-lucrative Welsh coal traffic. This also hit the export market through the dock system and the loss became permanent!

One practical, brighter feature of the 1920s was the C&W Works introduction of third-class sleeping cars, in tandem with the LMS and LNER companies, a move which proved very popular all round. A further bright spot taking us into the 1930s was the completion of the large (No. 24) Carriage Shop, 600ft x 400ft, one feature of which was production of the various paints required by the company. (A set of statistics produced in 1937 records show that the paint mill produced 1,000,000lbs of wagon paint, 900,000lbs of carriage paint, 20,000lbs of 'stopping' and 30,000lbs of timber filling.) It should also be noted that there was a considerable falling-off of repair work on rolling stock at this depression time, so the new No. 24 Shop was only half used for a lengthy period. Also, in spite of short-time working, some special large bogie wagons and a new 'super saloon' carriage design were produced. A serious fire in the Carpenters' Shop caused a rebuild of the original 1868 Lifting Shop in 1935.

It was also in the early 1930s that the steam rail motors of Great Western chugged their sorry way to their demise, outside the A Shop complex, some to be replaced by a small number of diesel-powered versions, the bodies not Swindon-made but supplied by the Gloucester Carriage & Wagon Co., and maintained by the maker so that virtually no work on these came to Swindon!

The end of the 1930s saw the last construction controlled by the finance arrangements. This was a very big structure covering 5 acres, which measured 1,800ft x 122ft. This structure covered additional built-up ground at the western extremity of the already built-up area, requiring 35,000 wagonloads of transported material from other excavations in several areas of the Great Western system. The area had been part of the local authority recreation ground exchanged for the land of the Great Western-owned park.

The idea was to store up to 265 carriages under one huge roof, the total area of which made the whole works probably the largest in Britain and possibly the greatest anywhere in the world – a good site for the storage of the new ambulance trains on the six rail lines the length of the Shop. As will be seen from the plans of the Works layout, the large amount of glass required 'blacking out' by painting over – a colossal task! And so war production pushed the whole Works back to square one, with the Carriage Works now possibly more involved with war production. As an office boy, I remember unofficially sitting on the 'human torpedo' or 'two-man submarine' behind a screen in the Finishing Shop, sited just outside the foreman's office. Other of the Shops making 'invasion barges' in the Wagon Frame Shop, the No. 24 Shop taken over by Messrs Short Bros Ltd for aircraft production. The Locomotive Works, dealing with the usual guns, shells and bombs (carcases not filled), was also pushed back to square one.

Maintenance of buildings continued if considered essential, and one great benefit was the changeover of the gas lighting to electricity, already on a programme but speeded up due to the war and the fact that the shops were completely blacked out anyway. I remember, this time as an apprentice, the electrification of the lathes and machine tools, individual motors applied in place of the long lines of flapping belts and overhead shafting.

In 1947, use of the new Carriage building was resumed. This was also the year in which the Great Western Railway was amalgamated into British Rail (Western Region). Thus began the demolition of a well established organisation and the introduction of mainly hybrid locomotives but as previously stated, C&W didn't change very much, as what was carried was 'the mixture as before'. It appeared that, in the reorganisation during nationalisation, no one from the Great Western was given a senior executive position, a decision which was considered by Great Western employees as a slap in the face. As duelling is illegal there was nothing to be done, so even now there is still a chip on the shoulder of Great Western enthusiasts! Whilst the Great Western and hybrid steam locomotives faded into history, soon to be followed by the Great Western diesel hydraulics, the Swindon Works floundered on.

A change in thinking had occurred in the 1950s and consultants were employed to look at costings, organisation and methods. This was certainly a burst of forward thinking due, in part, to union opposition to any question of a check on locomotive side-working procedures and productivity and lack of any backup from top management. Even a quick look into the C&W Works still met with opposition so that the Works, as a whole, managed to flounder on! (I was one of five employees initially seconded to the consultants for training and application of the techniques required.) The consultants thus moved out, along with the team, to work in the region, and the Loco Works were not investigated. There was a brief period in the C&W Works when a 'production control' scheme was proposed for a section making various components with a proposal for the storage and issue of items associated. Included was an examination of the costing and recording procedures with proposals for new paperwork, but such proposals were not pushed or expanded by using the consultants employed specifically for the purpose.

The Locomotive and C&W Works were in need of modernisation, but to cope with the completely different workloads required in an ex-steam-locomotive works and in the C&W Works, construction of all steel coaches introduced for example in 1950. By 1960, the chief mechanical and electrical engineers (CM&EE) independently had produced a 'General Plan for the future of Swindon Works'. There were thirteen proposals for the Locomotive Works and eleven for the C&W Works and for other shops' individual areas, the modernisation of which constituted a fifteen-year plan.

Not strictly carriage or locomotive, a new Points Crossings Shop was constructed with extensive equipment, size of Workshop and large storage yard. For the C&W Works, a new Steam Plant, Oil Works (No. 22 Shop) and an Oxygen Plant. Multiple-unit diesel engines were to be maintained in a completely rehashed 'B' Shed in the Loco Works and similar alterations for the change of locomotives in the 'A' Shop complex.

Changes in the C&W Works included a complete modernisation of the Wheel Shop (No. 16) with new lathes, craneage etc., and the installation of special lifting jacks and a new three-road extension for maintaining the diesel multiple units. A large 68ft carriage traverser covering the now thirty-two roads was installed, this now eliminated shunting problems. A new dynamometer test car was authorised and filled with the latest testing equipment, later to be transferred in this case to Derby, as the Motive Power Department was removed to Paddington. Although a new Apprentice Training School had been opened at Swindon, the thoughts were 'What other work was likely to be transferred somewhere else?' Again an example of too little, too late!

For the moment the introductions of the 'Blue Pullmans' with their double-end power units gave Swindon something else to consider, later followed by the high-speed trains (HST). Bogie design came under scrutiny and a new design was introduced – another thing to be transferred elsewhere, in this case to Derby and another production feature was lost. A new design of carriage to use the new bogie design was commenced at Swindon and this also was transferred later to Derby.

It was obvious change was coming, and in 1962 a number of main workshops were transferred to a new grouping as the 'Workshop Division of BR'. This was considered too hasty a move (lack of forward thinking again) and so we find later in 1962 yet another plan evolved as the Main Workshops Future Plan – yet another re-hash with the thirty-one main workshops slashed to sixteen. Among the fifteen to go, Swindon's Carriage & Wagon Works was to be totally closed. Again, Swindon Works had lost out! So all those years of development from 1868 were seemingly for nothing. The spirit was not dead, however, because whatever was left allocated to Swindon was to be transferred into redundant steam workshops in the Loco Works, which already had the diesel locomotive engine units under repair in what had been the long Iron Foundry building.

Maintenance work reduced all round. In the C&W Works, the new diesel multiple units, along with new design carriages meant, at least for a period, that work was getting very scarce. From a workforce of about 15,000 during the steam years (and the last steam locomotive *Evening Star* had been completed in 1960), the workforce had reduced by about one third.

The last CM&EE, Mr R. Smeddle, had retired and a new string of names came to fill the vacant equivalent post, no longer classed as CM&EE. A group of 'foreign' names from other railway works were to step into the posts vacated, and there was a general feeling that the intention was to close the Works. Work was now being obtained from wherever it could be found. Some locos, 0-6-0s, were being completed, but for the newly sited C&W, there were no more new carriage orders and by 1967 the total staff in the Works had reduced to just over 5,000.

One of the earliest workshops, the 'B' Shed, was now the Multiple Unit Lifting and Repair Shop. The scheme for a new carriage repair and lifting shop inevitably fell through. The complete area was now becoming a potential commercial site with one building, the Mechanics' Institute, which had held the first library in Swindon, now designated for a museum. Even the Great Western Gas Works had shut down and gas was now obtained from the local authority.

During 1977, another reorganisation was in the offing and some specialist work was undertaken for the Advanced Passenger Train (APT), which tilted as it traversed a curve. A distinct feature, actually one of two, was that the coach-body design included a distinct narrowing as it progressed up toward the roof, this keeping it inside the loading gauge as it tilted. A second feature really perpetuated another problem of eighty years before with the steam rail motor: the train comprised two 'units' of three coaches which were articulated, thus a problem with one affected the complete unit, taking half a train out of service.

A complete change of railway policy was introduced in which the whole was now affected by the removal of the longstanding restriction that the Railway Works (all of them not just Swindon) could enter the commercial marketplace and make things for sale to outside companies. Yet again, really too little, too late, the staff having rejected the hoped-for modernisation as promised by consultants in the 1950s. So began a scrappy period of odd jobs: the repair of diesel bus engines; a quickly accepted order for 'platform trolleys' (of all things); and a 'pie-in-the-sky' order for the complete refurbishment of Southern Region electric multiple-unit stock (and the sting in the tail) over a ten year period. This job was contracted to an Austrian firm for single and double jib track-laying crane frames, spread over four years. An order for twenty small diesel-hydraulic locomotives for Kenya. Staff were down to about 4,000 and continued to reduce! It couldn't go on – six years into the 1980s the complete Works shut down and the area is now a shopping mall and a museum still utilising some of the workshop buildings; much was already demolished.

Last one out turn off the lights and close the gates! What Brunel's comments would be I hate to imagine!

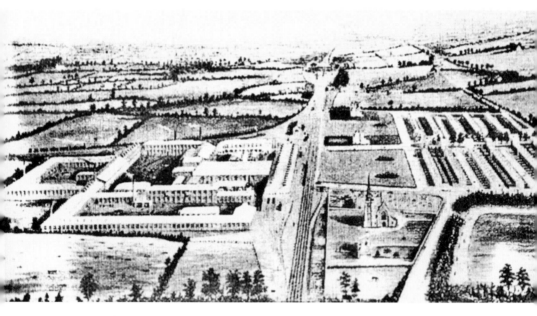

New Swindon in 1846: Swindon Works.

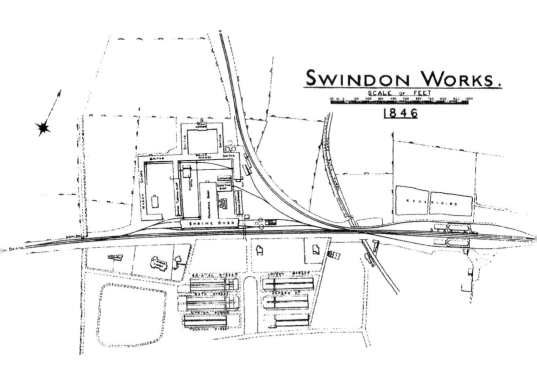

Swindon Works: railway housing estate.

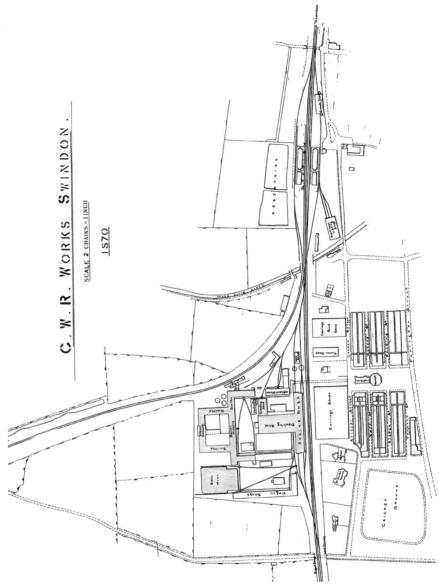

C. W. R. WORKS SWINDON.

SCALE 2 CHAINS = 1 INCH

1870

GWR Works Swindon, 1870.
Scale: 2 chains – 1 inch.

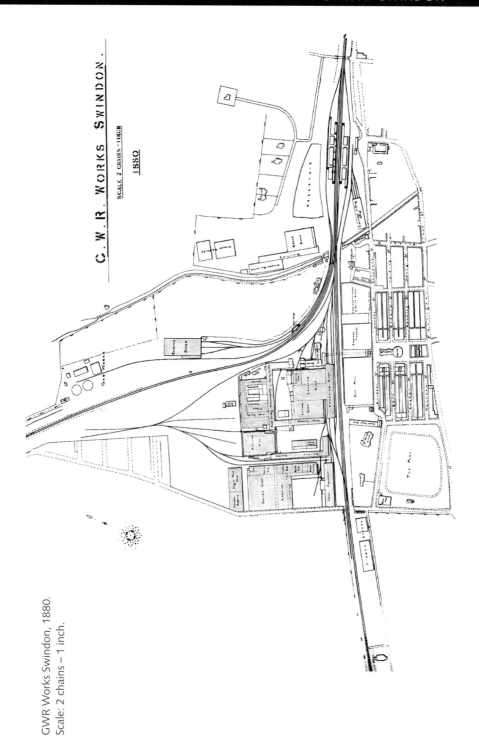

GWR Works Swindon, 1880.
Scale: 2 chains – 1 inch.

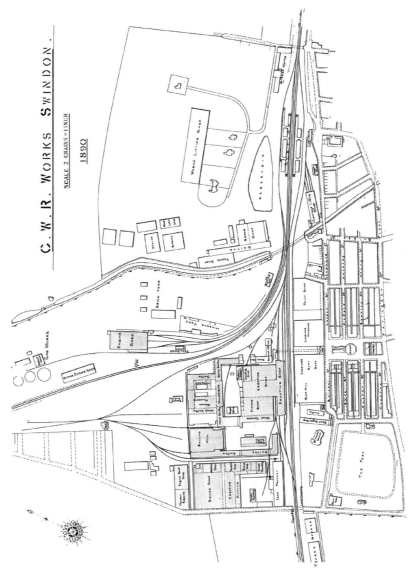

GWR Works Swindon, 1890.
Scale: 2 chains – 1 inch.

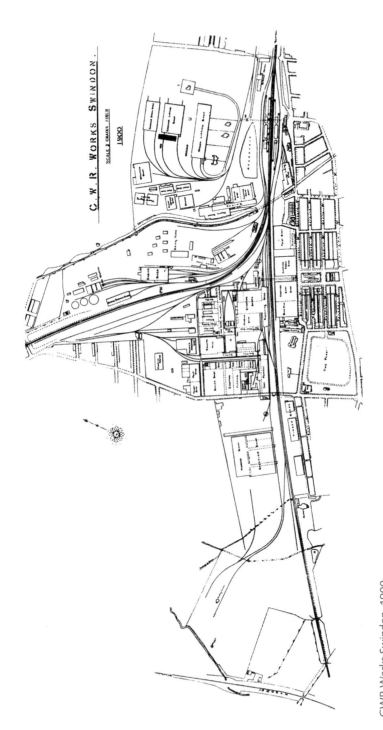

GWR Works Swindon, 1900.
Scale: 2 chains – 1 inch.

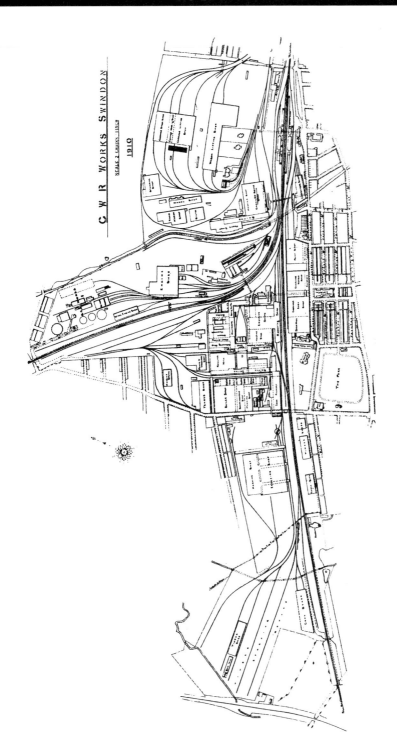

GWR Works Swindon, 1910.
Scale: 2 chains – 1 inch.

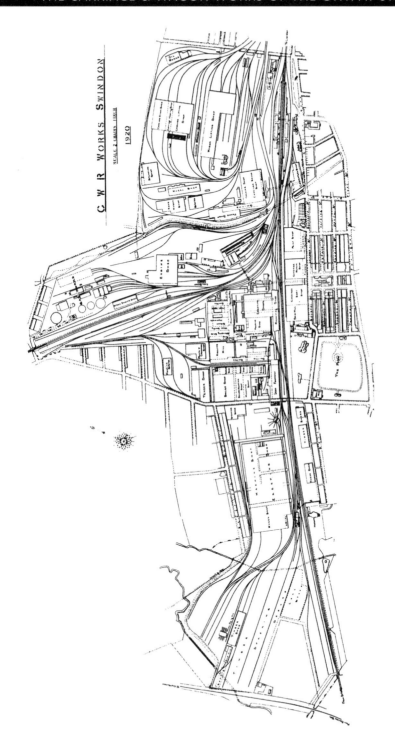

GWR Works Swindon, 1920.
Scale: 2 chains – 1 inch.

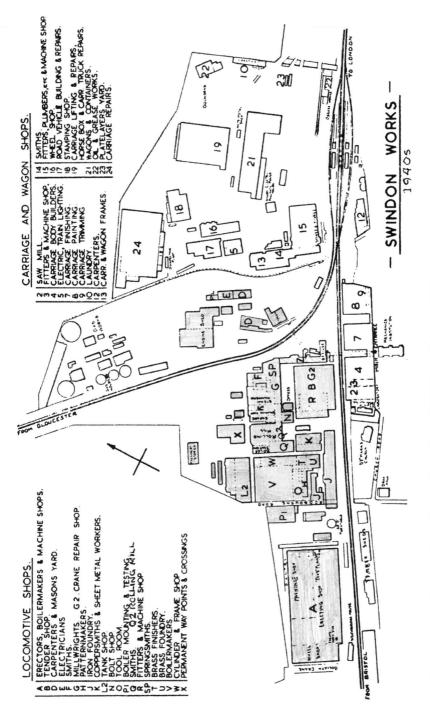

LOCOMOTIVE SHOPS.

A   ERECTORS, BOILERMAKERS & MACHINE SHOPS.
B   TENDER SHOP.
D   CARPENTERS & MASONS YARD.
E   ELECTRICIANS.
F   SMITHS.
G   MILLWRIGHTS.   G2. CRANE REPAIR SHOP.
H   PATTERNMAKERS.
J   IRON FOUNDRY.
K   COPPERSMITHS & SHEET METAL WORKERS.
L2 TANK SHOP.
N   BOLT SHOP.
O   TOOL ROOM.
P1 BOILER MOUNTING & TESTING.
Q   SMITHS.   Q2 ROLLING MILL.
R   FITTERS & MACHINE SHOP.
SP SPRINGSMITHS.
T   BRASS FINISHERS.
U   BRASS FOUNDRY.
V   BOILERMAKERS.
W   CYLINDER & FRAME SHOP.
X   PERMANENT WAY POINTS & CROSSINGS.

CARRIAGE AND WAGON SHOPS.

2   SAW MILL.
3   FITTERS & MACHINE SHOP.
4   CARRIAGE BODY BUILDERS.
5   ELECTRIC TRAIN LIGHTING.
7   CARRIAGE FINISHING.
8   CARRIAGE PAINTING.
9   CARRIAGE TRIMMING.
10 LAUNDRY.
11 CARPENTERS.
13 CARR. & WAGON FRAMES.
14 SMITHS.
15 FITTERS, PLUMBERS, etc. & MACHINE SHOP.
16 WHEEL SHOP.
17 ROAD VEHICLE BUILDING & REPAIRS.
18 STAMPING SHOP.
19 CARRIAGE LIFTING & REPAIRS.
    HORSE BOX & CARR. TRUCK REPAIRS.
21 WAGONS & CONTAINERS.
22 OIL & GREASE WORKS.
23 PLATELAYERS YARD.
24 CARRIAGE REPAIRS.

— SWINDON WORKS —
1940s

Swindon Railway Works in the Great Western Steam Years: GWR Works Swindon, 1940s.

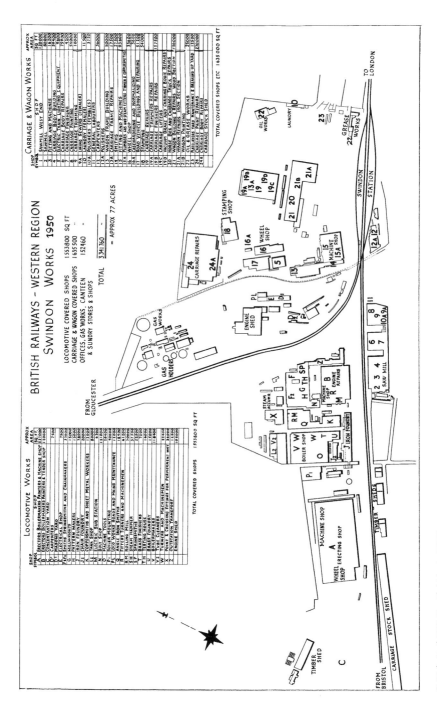

British Rail WR South West, 1950.

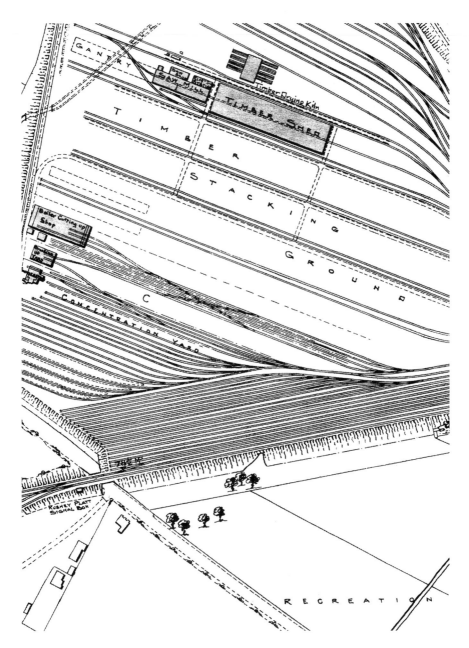

The Carriage and Wagon Works, western end, 1956.

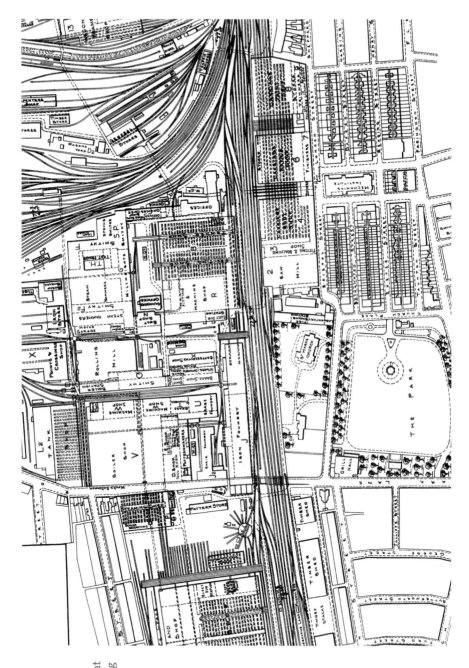

Central Carriage Works Section, 1956. This side of the main line, also showing the Great Western's housing estate.

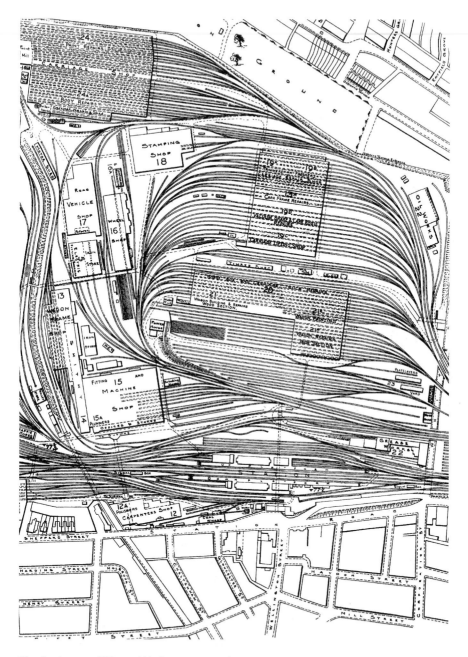

The Carriage and Wagon Works, eastern end, 1956.

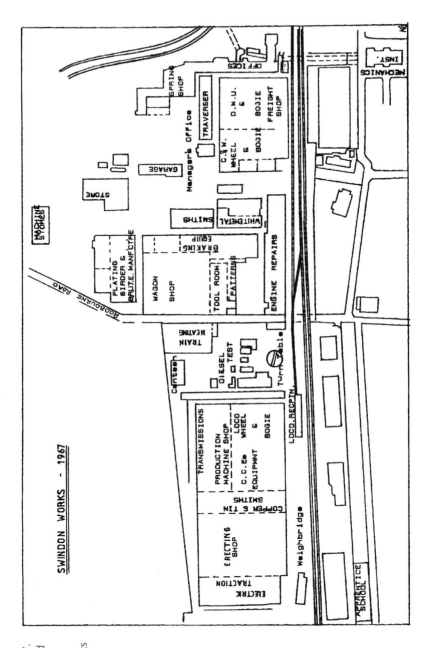

Swindon Works, 1967. By this date steam had gone and so had half the Swindon Works. The Locomotive Works area now included the remnants of the carriage and wagon operations.

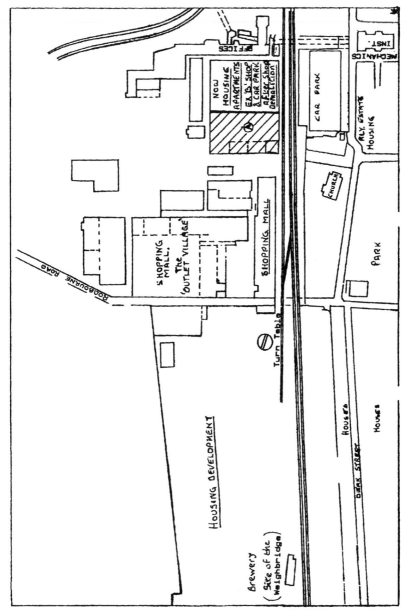

GWR Swindon Works, 2014. The structures that remain standing have an uncertain future, although some are protected. The shaded area is now STEAM, the railway museum centre for the GWR. The 'Works' has returned almost to its 1843 area.

THE GWR CARRIAGE AND WAGON WORKS AT SWINDON

Before embarking on a voyage through Swindon's Great Western Railway Carriage & Wagon workshops, it is important to know details of what was actually dealt with in the workshops visited. Therefore, the following pages guide the reader through the various design developments of the carriages and wagons and other associated items eventually made and maintained in the workshops illustrated.

Carriages of a sort, and the inevitable wagons, existed long before the Swindon Works, before settling into designs we now all recognise. In the early years these were made by private companies, contracted by the railways before they had the facilities to undertake the work themselves. Hence, the Great Western Railway's own C&W Works, where everything constructed, inherited or repaired had to conform to known, acknowledged 'weights and measures', and safety limits.

The design will be recognised as the carriage shown in the illustration of the inaugural run of the Stockton & Darlington Railway in 1825. How comfortable or otherwise the ride was is not recorded! Note the extended frame to act as 'buffers', the iron steps and the double chain 'couplings'. With no platform or station, and no handrails, getting aboard must have been difficult.

A first design: the first railway passenger carriage. Note the 'Venetian Blind' unglazed windows and the road wagon type wheels. The axles were fixed, and there were no springs.

CARRIAGE AND WAGON DESIGN

The design of transport for conveying passengers and goods or freight has several conditioning factors. Any design has to conform to the physical requirements of that which has to be transported. With the human passenger the size and shape of the human being is basically 'standard', within a narrow range of weight, height and width, and whatever is designed has to fit into the criteria of what became the 'loading gauge' in terms of mobility and safety, for the transport of passengers. Thus the shape and size of the passenger carriage has, no matter how elaborately 'furnished' inside or out, remained virtually standardised throughout the world, to accommodate 'standardised' passengers, carrying more as capacities were increased as development progressed. Differing from the human passenger, the transport of goods, whilst conforming to the 'loading gauge', covers a very wide range of sizes and weights and thus a wide range of general and specialist wagons has developed over the years.

Before the introduction of steam, the horse was the motive power, pulling loads with which it could readily cope, in little wagons full of stone and coal over very basic tracks, beginning with wood strip rails, it being easier to pull heavy loads on such tracks than on the muddy or dusty roads of the period. Probably the first human passengers were the drivers of the horses, sitting on the empty wagons on the return journey along the tramroad or plateway from the nearest canal and back to the mine or quarry.

By the time George Stephenson had proved the viability of the steam locomotive, transport that utlilised such a power source was well established as shown in the previous illustration on page 40, although comfort of the general passenger was certainly questionable!

So, the 'modern' transport world, which the Great Western entered in the 1830s and 1840s, had already established itself and the emergent requirements had also established a range of specialist vehicles to transport such requirements.

As noted by D. Clark, such vehicles form an interesting record of the period:

PASSENGER TRAIN STOCK	GOODS TRAIN STOCK
1. First-Class Carriage	Platform Wagon
2. Second-Class Carriage	Open-Box Wagon
3. Third-Class Carriage	High-sided Round End Wagon
4. Composite Carriage	Covered-Goods Wagon
5. Luggage Van	Cattle Wagon
6. Horse Box	Sheep Wagon
7. Carriage Truck	Coal Wagon
8. Fourth-Class Carriages	Coke Wagon
9. Brake Van	

Plus Specials for Gunpowder, Lime, Ballast etc. usually privately owned.

The composite carriage combined usually first and second classes, occasionally second and third classes, and often a luggage compartment was merged with the guards' brake van. The coke wagon was particularly important as many locomotives of the period burned coke. Local byelaws in the vicinity of the railway often forbade the emission of smoke from the locomotive, and coal, some types worse than others, gave considerable smoke, with the local law instructing that 'the loco should burn its own smoke.' This was very difficult, hence the insistence on the use of almost smoke-free coke, which had to be regularly transported to all locomotive depots on the growing system, as well as amounts of coal for internal and sale use.

PASSENGER TRAIN STOCK

A major problem in carriage design was not only in the design of the frame itself but the positioning of the wheels and wheel base to ensure correct support to avoid 'hogging', in which the wheels are too close together allowing the carriage to droop at the ends and rise in the centre. At this period many carriage manufacturers used wood framing, often reinforced by iron plates, but it is recorded that the Great Western of this period was already using complete frames of riveted wrought iron. This design enabled the frame to carry the full strain of all the stock behind it without problems. It was also recommended that once satisfactorily designed, all carriage frames whatever the class of body above, should be of uniform construction for standard ease of maintenance and construction – certainly good thinking.

Those first- and second-class carriages, which had upholstered seats, were also subjected to proposals, recorded as follows (in this current day and age rather humorously!):

As regards upholstery arrangements, it would be a great advantage to make them all moveable. The ordinary mode of trimming with cloth and wool, involves a large crop of moths, and is moreover a recipient for nuisance from the breaths of closely shut up passengers, which is not easily got rid of! Moreover the seats and stuffing which are agreeable in winter are uncomfortable in summer and vice-versa. The Railway Carriage in its structure should be regarded as an unfurnished apartment, and the furniture should be separate, and put in as required.

So much for the thought of carriage designers in the 1840s.

Whilst some carriages and wagons are detailed as development examples, this book is not a record of the many designs of rolling stock which evolved, often as improved 'marks' of a particular design, but of the development of the workshops which undertook the work, from the adaptation, as we have seen, of coal and coke wagons for passenger use, from the four-, six- and eight-wheel designs, through to the double four- and six-wheel bogie designs, with examples through the years as well as examples of the construction and progress of wagon design.

In the mid-1850s two items, which appear out of place in the passenger-train list are Nos 6 & 7, the Horse Box and the Carriage Wagon. Nos 6 & 7 were specialist wagons which carried the road carriages of the well-to-do, as well as their horses, with possibly grooms, maids and footmen etc. ensconced in the third-class carriages whilst the owners travelled first class. It is recorded that 'fourth-class carriages are still in use on some lines'. What sort of accommodation was afforded by a fourth-class carriage is not recorded but we may assume pretty basic (and suitable for maids and grooms).

The carriage wagon or truck was a flat bed designed to support a road carriage and having 4ft-diameter wheels positioned outside the body, a design which was to lead to much comment and discussion before the Gauge Commission in due course. (Wheel position was not a problem with broad gauge.) The design was really a way of securing a wheeled road vehicle on top of a wheeled rail vehicle with large diameter wheels. We must always bear in mind that we are talking about broad-gauge vehicles, so there was enough room to mount a road carriage, which wouldn't have been so easy on the 4ft 8½in gauge! There appears to have been a surfeit of upper-crust families in the Great Western area who requested that they travel in their own carriage, so it was not always empty carriages that were being transported. Thus there was quite a demand for such facilities at a number of stations for loading onto the wagons. There were also a considerable number of carriage trucks: 161 in 1845 and an increase to 224 in the next four years. Regarding the sizes, Gooch's evidence before the gauge commissioners in 1845 contained the emphatic assurance that the road coaches 'fitted completely inside the wheels with no overhang!'

Although the fit onto the wagons appears satisfactory, there is no mention of the effect on the 'loading gauge' for tunnels and bridges clearance on a fully loaded carriage, complete with the family enjoying their privacy. Thus there were probably routes which could not be used although there appears to be no mention of any such problems.

As with period railway carriages, many followed the road-vehicle design with a seat on top at the end for a 'guard'. Also a number followed the road carriage with the roof used for carrying the luggage!

The horse box of the broad gauge of this early period was a very strong design, and, according to the comments of George Stephenson when facing the Gauge Commission: 'I have observed upon that line that the motion of the Horse Boxes is sometimes fearful, from the side-to-side motion because they want length with reference to their width.' It was also noted that the horses travelled sideways, four to a box. The horse box was wider at 10ft 8in than it was long at 9ft 8in x 7ft 6in. With 3ft-diameter wheels at 6ft centres, it must have been very unstable. Longer and narrower vehicles were later designed for three horses facing the box ends. With four horses sideways, they also must have been as uncomfortable as the passengers!

The railway carriage, whilst certainly in the early years seemingly a reluctant necessity to the railway companies, certainly reflected the class structure of the Victorians. We have seen, at the beginning of this book, the adaptation of open coal and coke wagons for 'the rest', whilst the directors and proprietors of the railway had the covered benefit of what looks like a garden shed on wheels!

The Great Western, having opened its Works at Swindon, had a wagon building workshop but there is no mention of carriage building at this early stage. When it did start 'construction', it concentrated on the chassis, the bodywork 'farmed out' to several coach makers. These were the road-vehicle constructors, and their influence is certainly reflected in the designs. So conditioned were they to the road coach-design format that some carriage designs looked like several road-coach bodies joined together. Some manufacturers even included an outside seat for a guard, high up on the coach end. (Whether there was a 'mind your head' notice for bridges and tunnels is not recorded!) Fortunately the 'high seat' addition does not appear to have been inflicted on the Great Western although there was an 'iron coffin' arrangement on the back of the tender of some locomotive designs where an unfortunate 'guard' sat to keep an eye open and tell the driver if the train broke in half due to a failed coupling!

Private carriage constructors continued to build for the Great Western for a number of years. These early builders are listed as follows:

Beard
D. Davies (First Class Carriages) of London
Dell
Gower
Mather & Chantler
R. Melling and Co. of Manchester (the First Class Carriages)
J Perry
W. Shackleford, with works at Benson near Wallingford and Cheltenham
Williams

Four-wheel carriages were in general use in the first years, but as early as 1837 Brunel forwarded proposals for six wheelers, arranging for some ordered with four wheels to be altered to the new standard. Four-wheeled vehicles did not immediately vanish however, the last two not going until 1862. Gooch himself had also criticised four-wheel carriages as 'derailing easily because they were too light.' The second-class carriage was also the subject of severe criticism. Shown in the following illustration, it had no glazed windows, just large openings and passengers could be soaked by driving rain, or frozen by sleet or snow. The 'seconds' were removed from service in 1844. How the third- and fourth-class passengers suffered can only be imagined! Things had to improve.

The first appearance of Swindon-built passenger vehicles were Luggage Vans, both body and chassis of iron credited to Gooch in 1844, following an order for complete wooden vehicles to be made by Braby & Carr, employed at Paddington. Third-class passengers graduated in 1845 from the open truck vehicles to what almost appeared to be prison vans – all iron sheets on angle iron frames with very tiny windows high up in the doors only. Presumably the passengers 'talked among themselves' as it was difficult to see anything going on in the passing countryside whilst seated! (These vehicles were converted in about 1860 to Luggage Vans.) Seating was in the now-common 'across the width' as opposed to around the walls, in normal compartments as the only division was the seat backs.

A turn away from iron frames occurred around 1847, when a number of wood-framed carriages were built, the bodies by the outside firms of David Davis of London, Messrs Wright of Salney and Shackleford Co. as well as a batch by the Great Western at Paddington using iron frames by Hennet Co.

In 1846 Brunel insisted that a mechanically trained person should be in charge of C&W maintenance and repairs and in 1846 Mr J. Gibson was appointed Superintendent of the C&W Department.

During the 1850s what appears to be a strange experiment, which proved successful, was undertaken. We have seen coach panels made of wood and iron but not papier mâché! This idea being accepted, during the 1850s, the panelling of all first, second, and composite builds were to be of this material. The builders were Messrs Wright of Birmingham, Shackleford now at Cheltenham, J. Ward of Exeter and Perry & Co. of Wolverhampton. During a period of seven years, the Great Western built some at Paddington. A number of iron frames were made at Swindon, with a number on contract to Ashbury of Manchester.

The continuing growth and acceptance of railway travel inevitably led to a continuation of the seemingly 'them and us' view regarding travel facilities. Open-type or 'prison-van' conveyances for third-class passengers led to the inevitable backlash from the travelling pubic, with complaints registering in high places, many of whom were firmly of the opinion that this was done to persuade those complaining to upgrade to the more costly second or first class. When the secretary of the company appeared before the Parliamentary Committee in 1839, he suggested that perhaps the Company would concede cheap fares, at low speed, once a day in 'inferior stock', possibly at night! Such an idea proved unacceptable!

In 1844 Gladstone, then President of the Board of Trade, introduced a bill, which became law, that there should be a daily train, third class for a penny a mile, with good seating arrangements, with good ventilation and light. The railway companies soon found a way of 'driving a coach and horses' through the act so this type of travel, akin to 'coal and coke wagons', changed very little. So with carriages with hard wood seats, shutters instead of glazed windows or just open-sided with a roof, and Venetian type ventilators for the 'good ventilation and light' either open or closed, the Act was satisfied! There had been a case so recorded that a passenger in one of the lower standard of carriages had actually succumbed to the cold and frozen to death. So much for the class system!

1852 saw the introduction of the first eight-wheeled rolling stock, specifically for regular express passenger services, the first in Britain, and of course broad gauge. These longer vehicles, quickly nicknamed 'Long Charleys' – at 38ft, these were not 'bogie' designs. They had wood bodies by Shackleford and iron frames constructed at Swindon. Detailed information on vehicles is limited to preliminary designs with pencilled in modifications, one showing a large spring supported on the fulcrum of the beam with hangers outside the horns at each end of the four-wheel arrangement, with equalised attachment to weighty compensating beams between the pair. There was limited side play by a pivotal action of the assembly of the whole with 4ft-diameter wheels. The wheels at 4ft were on fixed axles, so there was no way the 'bogie' appearance could swivel as they projected upwards through the floor of the carriage, protected by the usual 'splashers'. These were composite coaches and had four second- and three first-class compartments, with seating for twelve seats per compartment second class and eight seats for first class. Although the first bogie-style carriages to make the eight-wheel format, these were not the first-eight wheel carriage designs. It appears that the quest for opulence was directed generally at the Royals, with companies vying with each other to prepare the most elaborate vehicles. In the quest for such a vehicle for Queen Victoria, the eight wheeler came to the fore to replace an original which had been decorated with carved furniture, silk hangings and with classic scenes painted on the ceiling. Originally a four-wheel design following the 'Posting' carriage classification was decreed to be unstable, so the eight-wheel new frame was substituted. This was replaced by a further eight wheeler in 1849, again not a bogie vehicle which, over its lifetime, was rebuilt several times to drastically alter its appearance.

An earlier Royal coach had a disc-type signal on top of the roof, operated from inside, which was intended to pass instructions to the (unfortunate) occupier of the 'iron coffin' for him to pass on to the driver – the iron box mounted on the back of the locomotive's tender facing back down the train. This unenviable individual's job was to keep a sharp lookout for the occasion, occurring too often, when a coupling broke and the train separated, particularly in the early years when there were no continuous brakes to clamp on when the situation arose, and there were probably only one or two guards seated among third class-passengers, with a wheel in front of them which, on turning, applied the brakes on the individual carriage. (An example is shown on page 53.) Whilst in the Royal Carriage there was, at least in the later design, a 'toilet' compartment. It was to be some years before such a facility became a standard design fitting, so drinking that second cup of tea before boarding was certainly not advisable!

In 1872 the Midland Railway accepted a contract for the use of the American 'Pullman' car on their lines – one early example of private enterprise on the railways of Britain (the Americans at this time were running over 700 on their railways). The contract was for fifteen years; the Midland supplying 'motive power, warmth and protection', and the Pullman Company agreeing to supply 'the cars in good order with suitable attendants'. For this service the Midland charged a first-class fare; the Pullman Company 'a certain very moderate additional sum'. One statement recorded that 'The Pullman car costs no less than £3,000, a sum nearly equal to the travelling carriage built by the London & North Western Company for the use of the Queen'.

The following illustrations help to show the astonishingly rapid growth in design over a period of about thirty years, from the carriage's introduction in America in the 1860s. These six-wheel double-bogie vehicles show an exceptional level of opulence, described as 'Exquisitely carpeted, upholstered and furnished, pivoted chairs, crimson cushioned …' Nowhere was this more true than in the six-wheel swivelling bogies.

The introduction of the American 'Pullman Car' to British lines triggered a desire to have more elaborate decoration and internal layout within British carriages. It also inspired a move into the realm of the real 'sleeping' car, with the advent of some very strange designs by Continental railways. The Great Western stepped into the sleeper design contest in 1877 for overnight use between Paddington and Penzance. The design of their first two included washing and toilet facilities as well as beds but in such tight formation that passengers remarked they felt 'like cod on a fishmonger's slab!' This design lasted until the late 1880s when these carriages were then converted to family saloon-type vehicles in part due to the objections of the first-class travelling public.

Another design feature greatly influenced by the American Pullman car was the introduction of the 'clerestory' roof in the late 1870s. Several different designs of clerestory roof sprouted up in Britain, all of which derived from the original Pullman car design. Whilst it gave raised space for the early lighting arrangements, particularly the first oil and then gas lamps, and questionable extra daylight from the little windows along the length (when cleaned!), as well as allowing passengers in top hats to walk unrestricted down the centre of the coach, it certainly complicated the structure of the carriage roof.

The usual curved roof was supported at regular intervals with substantial 'roof hoops', secured at each end to the carriage sides, and here and there with a floor-to-ceiling panel separating compartments. The hoops were made in one piece, steamed for several hours and then bent around a 'former' (illustrated on page 123) on a special machine, allowed to cool and when released had acquired the permanent-curve roof shape.

The application to the design of the clerestory meant that a large chunk had to be removed from the centre of the roof level. This was replaced by a number of small vertical window frames – above the roof level and containing the raised roof section – which was itself cut out at regular intervals to accommodate access openings for the oil lamps or gas-light 'exhaust' gases. The few advantages of the clerestory roof were negated when on occasion the roof hoops were manufactured as a complete piece with the clerestory structure built on top of them.

Doubts were raised about the strength of its structure. Many feared what the consequences might be in the event of a crash. And, because of the many small components involved in the type of roof, a number of problems arose, including leakage along the roof rail, and regular maintenance of the structure meant much higher upkeep costs. Yet the design was popular – lasting about thirty years – during which time a number of railways hopped onto the bandwagon.

The Americans were quick to utilise the clerestory in their coaches but it was the Pullman that represented the zenith of the design. In Britain, as early as

1838, some of the posting coaches had a form of clerestory, but again it was the American Pullman that brought the clerestory to its completion.

Great Western's 1874 building programme included a new coach for Her Majesty. Whilst built as an eight-wheel standard gauge, not of the clerestory design, it was a favourite, as she never again travelled broad gauge – the eight-wheeler's frame was later altered to run on Dean's four-point suspension bogies. Around 1897 the coach underwent further modernisation, this time for bodywork lengthening. It survived to be used as a hearse car for the funeral of Edward VII, but was finally scrapped in 1912.

The 1874 building programme included a number of these eight wheelers; larger and larger vehicles with the eight wheels grouped four at each end, not as bogies. These carriages had Mansell wood-centre wheels, oil lamps, two in each compartment, and the clerestory roof design. The success of the Mansell wheel was such that very few original iron-spoked examples were still running past the 1890s. Standard-gauge eight wheelers were becoming the order of the day by the end of the 1870s, and by about 1905 the clerestory roof was fading from designs in favour of the rounded roof with which we are now familiar. As well as this, electric light was superseding gas lighting, the better quality of light supplanting the need for extra glazing in the roof.

Around 1905, the usual passenger coach length was increased with the introduction of a 70ft trailer car for the steam-rail motors. The new length was applied to four dining cars and ordinary passenger carriages – smoothly curved roofs and no clerestory silhouette! Later in the decade a change of bogie type was introduced, based on an American design, so the new longer coaches had 8ft, later 9ft, equalised bolster bogies, superseding the well established Dean design. One carriage which, built in 1901, retained its clerestory roof. This carriage strangely enough was built as a 'wagon' as a bit of a fiddle with budgets that allowed the expense to be carried by Wagon Lot 293! This was Churchward's 'dynamometer car', the special vehicle carrying the steam locomotive testing equipment. The vehicle could be regularly seen on test runs or, as a static laboratory, adjacent to the Locomotive Test Plant in the 'A' Shop complex at Swindon Works.

Quite a number of railways still had special 'saloon' versions being made well into the 1890s, with first-class seating around the sides and at the ends. These cars utilised the Mansell wood-centre wheel. In 1892, the Car Yard at Swindon was overflowing with broad-gauge coaches, in for scrapping or conversion depending on the type of body design. A number of these had been purposely made to standard-gauge format on broad-gauge frames and bogies but designed so that the body could be 'jacked up', the broad bogies lowered out and run out of the pit, and a pair of narrow bogies run under and connected (see page 57).

PASSENGER TRAIN VEHICLES OF THE 1840S

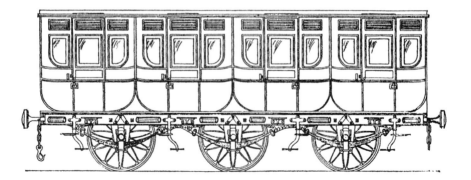

First-class carriage.

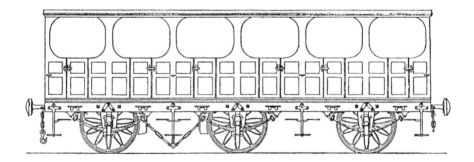

Second-class carriage. Note the unglazed windows and wheels under the bodies.

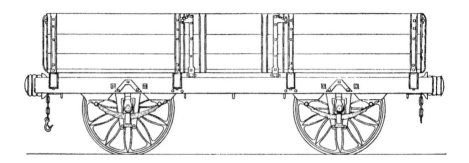

Third-class carriage.

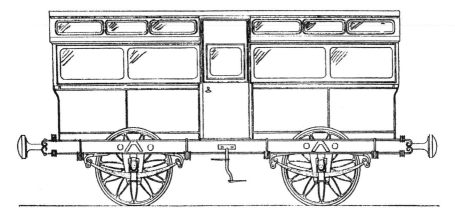

The 'Posting Carriage' had 'cushioned seats all round and a table down the middle' – it was calculated to hold eighteen persons. This would now be classed as a 'saloon' carriage.

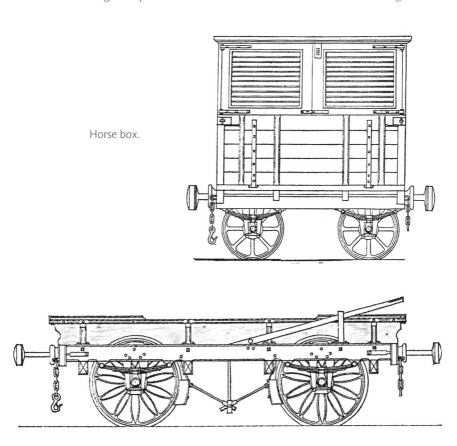

Horse box.

Carriage truck. Note the 4ft-diameter wheels outside the bodies in both the posting carriage and the carriage truck.

CARRIAGE UNDERFRAMES OF THE 1840S

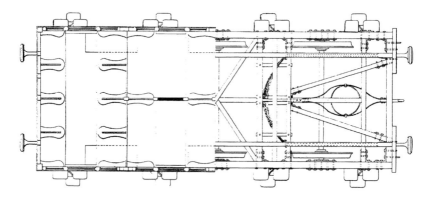

First-class carriage.

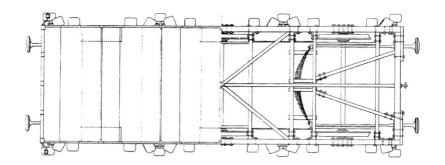

Second-class carriage.

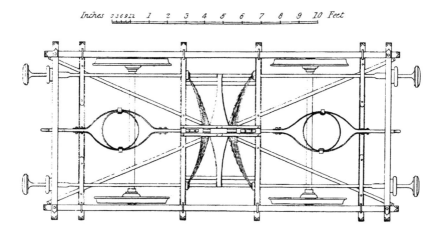

Posting carriage.

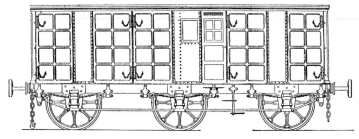

Passenger luggage van 1848 with guard's compartment (brake gear omitted).

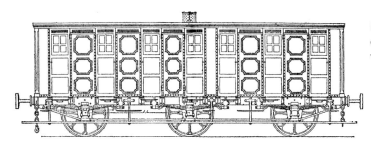

Iron third-class carriage (side view), 1848.

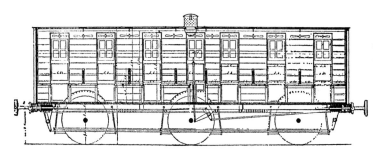

Iron third-class carriage (section), 1848.

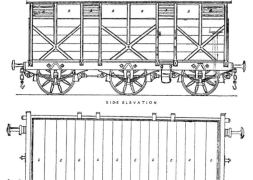

Third-class carriage 1844. Side elevation, transverse section and plan.

A   Fixed ventilators, or Venetians
B   Spaces to be open, or closed by sliding doors
C   Seats for six passengers each
D   Seat for five passengers each

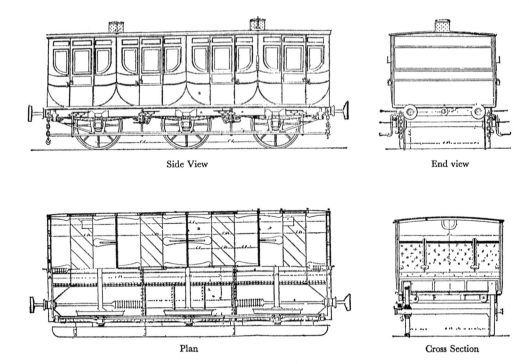

Side View

End view

Plan

Cross Section

First-class carriage, *c.* 1851: side view, end view, plan and cross section.

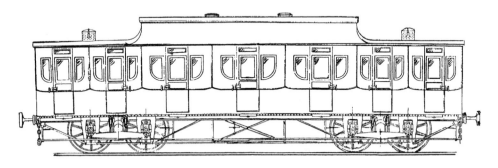

Eight-wheel broad-gauge composite carriage for the GWR Birmingham Service, 1852 (the 'Long Charleys').

A four-wheel survivor in the 1850s. Note the 'road carriage' design of the compartments.

A later 1850s version of the four-wheel coach from the previous illustration. This one has six-wheels but still with road-coach format compartments.

Pullman cars.

Interior of Pullman Car
Examples show the incredible development of the railway carriage compared with the
'travelling public' in the adapted coal and coke wagons used only forty years or so before
for the first journey on the Stockton & Darlington Railway shown at the beginning of
this book.

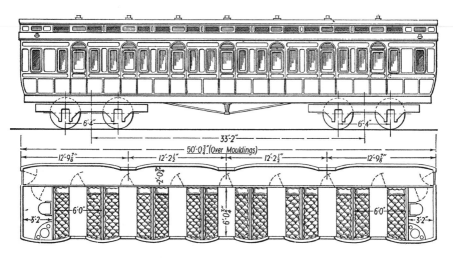

Dean's GWR broad-gauge convertible corridor sleeping car, 1890.

Swindon's Carriage Body Shop with a conversion in progress.

It is 1892 and the end of broad gauge. A mix of convertible wide-body and narrow-body coaching stock, and wide-body (not convertible) designs in the third row to be scrapped. There was also a similar area at Swindon for the associated sorting of the broad gauge convertible and non-convertible locomotives.

EXAMPLES OF GREAT WESTERN STEAM RAIL MOTORS 1903–1934

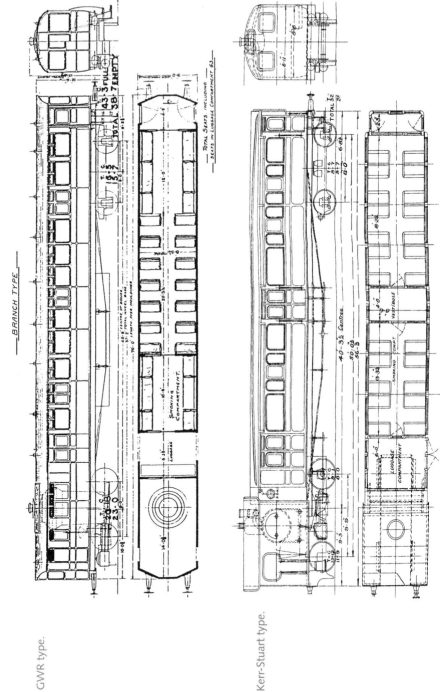

GWR type.

Kerr-Stuart type.

Coaches were now taking a form familiar to us all, irrespective of the variations in internal layout and design. Bogie construction was also a central focus of design. In 1888, Samson Fox, of the Leeds Forge Company, patented his modern pressed-steel bogie, as had been used on the Midland Railway. The Great Western stuck to tradition, continuing with William Dean's pendulum-link design of bogie, and building, from the 1870s to the early 1900s, the clerestory roof designs with a distinct shape on the ends for the installation of the concertina joint arrangement for access to the next carriage. This, for a now unknown reason, was also applied to some carriages without the central corridor, so that a complete rehash of the internal design of the carriage would have been required. Lighting was by now oil gas, and reservations continued on the potential of gas and the weakness of the clerestory design in the event of a crash and fire. Coal gas had been used, with two lamps in each first-class compartment, with the gas stored in special roof-mounted boxes and contained in rubber bags, weighted on top, so they collapsed and folded as the gas was used. Four-wheel coaches carried around 62 cubic ft of gas and eight-wheel coaches carried double that amount.

Electric lighting was first attempted in 1881. Cars had to be rebuilt, requiring a not insubstantial amount of work: 'Installation involved the setting-up a massive battery under the car of thirty-two 45½-lb Faurê [sic] cells, supplying current for twelve Swan (a famous name) incandescent lamps mounted on the lower section of the roof.' The battery 'was good for six hours'. On the whole, this was an elaborate and certainly weighty inclusion and the very fragile carbon–filament lamps gave a light probably equivalent to around half a dozen glow worms. Apparently in some sections of the coaches, the light was not strong enough for reading! However, it was a start, tempting Stroudley to equip four more cars. Carriage lighting was now considered in earnest; an 1876 introduction of oil gas by Julius Pintsch was tried out, the compressed oil-gas being carried under pressure in cylinders stored either within, under or over the carriages, giving a forty-hour supply that pushed the electrical approach into the background for a time.

During the 1880s experiments continued with separate electrical generators or pulley arrangements through the floor with belts to one of the axles. The Great Western, very late in development, actually went backwards! In the depth of the Railway Act of 1921, the Midland South Western Junction Railway had its horse boxes fitted with electric light, and as soon as the Great Western on amalgamation clapped eyes on them, it had the electrics stripped out and gas substituted! Gas lasted, with great determination, right into the 1940s, in spite of a recorded number of occurrences most feared by the opponents of clerestory roof stock, crashes and fires in gas-fitted stock.

The Great Western introduced its first corridor train in 1891, although consisting of only four coaches, one of each first, second and third class with a brake third, all with oil-gas lighting and clerestory roofs, with a 40ft non-corridor van at the tail end. This effort had been preceded in 1890 with a Dean design for a corridor coach in the form of a sleeping car and was in essence a narrow-gauge body on broad-gauge (temporary) bogies. This was a unique first idea, as the corridor continued at the side to an end door opening for a connecting 'concertina' bellows also at the side, an arrangement, which was found to be rather impractical if one coach was reversed on assembly of the train. With the 1891 four-coach train, with side corridors and end doors, only the guards had keyed access to the other coaches by means of the locked doors (reputedly stopping third-class travellers from surreptitiously creeping along to personal upgrade!). Passengers could summon the guard by electric bell push, or partially apply the brakes by tugging on a wire along the roofline. There was also a 'modern' first, with steam-heating pipework drawing steam from the locomotive. These coaches were also good examples of complete roof hoops across the width of the carriage, with the clerestory roof above sprouting from the hoops.

To the 'man-in-the-street' railway coaches in the steam years appeared to differ very little once the four- or six-wheel bogie had been introduced in the usual pairs. The enthusiast is adept at identifying the designer, year of build and subsequent 'marks' of the same basic design per railway company and can quote the main differences between the usual marks, but to many all coaches began to look the same! Certainly painted different colours for the different railway companies, but as long as time of journey, comfort and safety were known to exist it was of little or no interest in what design or mark of coach the journey was being made.

The major differences were changes in materials and methods of construction. We have seen different designs of bogie, wheel construction, braking systems, lighting, heating, iron replacing wood and then steel replacing iron. Axle design having the wheel revolving on the axle to the wheel firmly attached to the axle which itself revolves within first a grease-lubricated, then oil-lubricated 'axle box' right up to, eventually, trails with ball and then roller bearings. All unknown to the man-in-the-street as is the carriage and wagon frame, first of wood, then iron, then steel – first riveted then welded. All of which were important factors in the life of a Carriage & Wagon Works, especially to the craftsmen so trained and employed.

Whilst the absorption and takeover of other railway companies during the nineteenth century in the continued expansion of the Great Western had landed the company with narrow- or standard-gauge stock, the new century would be all 4ft 8½in gauge. The first forty or so years of the new century would bring about a period of turmoil unlike anything in the previous sixty years, in which two World Wars would be fought, and during which the demise of the Great Western was set motion.

The rapid development of the railway carriage had now reached a stage which we all now recognise easily: a maximum controllable length approaching about 70ft, with varying internal designs. Development continued, and at the turn of the century an innovation seemed to trigger great interest almost worldwide (possibly excluding the USA) taking the form of a self-propelled carriage, which became known as a steam-rail motor (SRM), a carriage with a steam engine built into one end. Whilst the interest spread across Britain's railways, it fired the greatest interest at the Great Western, which began building with great enthusiasm, designing and building ninety-seven of them, with slight variations to batches as they developed. The private manufacturer was not forgotten, a pair being purchased (why does not appear to be clarified), from Kerr-Stuart & Co. built to that company's design, although following a basic pattern. These all created somewhat of a dual-maintenance problem, as the detailed components were nothing like their Great Western equivalents. Most railway works had their two main functions – the locomotives and the carriage and wagon functions – separated. To maintain and service the steam engine meant siting the 'SRM' in a Running Shed, not really conducive to cleanliness for the coach. For the coach end, maintenance meant difficulties with the steam-engine end.

Although very successful in opening up the rural transport facilities of the Great Western, they were too successful, with more potential traffic than they could cope with. Whilst they could manage to pull a coach, there was not enough power for additional animal and farm traffic. Within ten years they were being converted to separate locomotive and carriage units, a small 0-6-0 or 0-4-2 locomotive capable of being detached and used for shunting other farm wagons to make up a short train – a job for which the steam rail motor was unsuited, both for manoeuvrability and power.

Retarded by the First World War, by 1934 the steam-rail motor on the Great Western was confined to the history books, having been progressively altered to trailer carriages, sold off, or scrapped.[1] A different, updated design by private manufacturers continued to thrive in other countries, Egypt and Cyprus being two such examples up to the end of the century. A rebuilt Great Western version is now running at Didcot and a three-car Egyptian unit is in the stages of a rebuild in England, both for heritage companies.

A first jolt to any feeling of complacency was the build-up to, and the commencement of the First World War, on 4 August 1914. Mention was made earlier of the increased pressures forced on the carriage builders by the additional requirements and skills, coupled with ingenuity, when the question of ambulance trains came to the fore. Listed on page 13 is the Carriage & Wagon management structure over the years and it was the shoulders of F.W. Marillier (1902–20) that bore the weight of requirements and design for the 1914–18 war-period requirements.

---

1. For a full story of the steam rail motor see my book entitled *The Steam Rail Motors of the Great Western Railway* (Stroud: History Press, 2015).

Among the many problems, was the fitting in of the necessary hospital ward bed accommodation in the capacity of a railway coach body, and whilst fitting in as many as possible within three-tier bunks, a major problem arose. To get wounded men from a carrying stretcher into the top bed, in particular, ran the risk of causing further injuries, especially to the severely wounded, and so one of the Marillier improvements was the design of folding frames with removable sections which would provide a fitted stretcher to help transfer the patient into bed. The bottom bunks could form seats for any sitting patients awaiting treatment. Among Marillier's other achievements were patented improvements to carriage lighting, axle boxes, train heating and the workshop procedures of forging coupling components.

As the orders for ambulance trains continued to flood in, so the internal design of the coaches included more actual 'living' facilities for staff and patients. Two major improvements included heating and electric lighting in place of the usual gas-oil energy source. The trains included accommodation for the medical staff with a very welcome kitchen facility, making a self-contained unit.

Some of the trains were for use in France and others for Britain, and it is recorded that, in 1915, a batch of four coaches destined for France were on a ship which was either mined or torpedoed in crossing the Channel, having not travelled very far before damage occurred. The ship, in sinking condition, was beached off the Kent coast, but in such a position that salvaging the coaches was not possible. There were fatal casualties but a trawler picked up the majority of the crew, while a skeleton crew continued to operate aboard the damaged vessel. Those rescued included the Great Western's personnel who were there to supervise the unloading of the carriages at their destination.

War requirements had certainly provided a great deal of extra production work for the C&W Works, including 638 ordinary passenger coaches as well as 238 specialist carriages for the sixteen completed ambulance trains, with nine to sixteen coaches per train. The earliest efforts had been conversions from other coach designs, including brake vans, which had begun even before the war started. The early versions had all the necessary facilities of wards, operating theatre, a pharmacy section, with accommodation for two doctors, two nurses and eight assistant orderlies. These first vehicles were for internal use, transferring wounded from the docks to various hospitals, and *Great Western Magazine* reported that, in December 1914, 135 patients were transported from Southampton to Bristol, followed by a second journey from Leith to Plymouth when a further 120 casualties and ambulance cases were moved from the North Sea Fleet. Despite the general feeling that it would all be over by Christmas, this situation continued for another four years, with the later years seeing the inclusion of wounded American allies as well.

THE AMBULANCE TRAIN REQUIREMENTS: A REPEAT OF THE FIRST WORLD WAR FOR THE SECOND WORLD WAR

A rapid end? It was not to be! And it was all to be repeated again twenty years later. Demand for specialist vehicles was again to be the priority from 1939 and, once again, requests for ambulance vehicles came to the fore. The pattern of work changed to additional special requirements, stripping out interiors of coaches, removing portions and compartments and installing wider doors where possible to assist with access for stretcher cases. As early as 1939 the Swindon Works received a contract for conversion of LMS carriages for ambulance train use.

The following couple of examples will give an idea of the new requirements of 1943, when the American orders were received. Additionally to the 'ward' carriage (conversions from Great Western milk vans), with their rows of beds, were the two 'support' vehicles, both conversions from existing corridor-brake thirds. These 57ft long vehicles were specifically converted for the US Army to their specification and are listed as diagrams 'F' and 'G', 'F' being the wound dressing and pharmacy facility and 'G' with boiler and hot water pumping equipment for the train (for heating when not coupled to the locomotive), and cupboards and shelves for medical stores. They were also fitted out with a padded compartment for those requiring special treatments. Other vehicles were fitted out for living accommodation for the medical staff. The train capacity, varying slightly depending on design, provided for approximately 230 stretcher cases and sitting accommodation for about sixty 'walking wounded', cared for by a varying number of medical staff totalling around forty per train.

From the early orders of 1939 for a total of fourteen ambulance trains, and as the conflict progressed beyond the 'all over by Christmas' forecast, further

Ambulance train coach.

orders were placed to increase the total to twenty-seven, which included the five specifically for our American allies. The vehicles were also to be operated by American military personnel. A whole train comprised a selection of around ten to twenty vehicles, both ambulance and support, with living and stores etc.

For virtually half of the twentieth century, the exigencies were of keeping things running up to, during, and after the conflict of the First World War and in the following period of short-time working, strikes, lay-offs, boom and bust economies. Just pulling itself back together, the Great Western was thrust into another upheaval with the Second World War, so the process repeated itself in great measure, and was eventually followed by nationalisation. For the previous fifty or so years, nothing had really changed – still steam hauled, at the same speeds, with the same stock, at the same timings; but that was soon to change. New thinking was in the air. Why not have a general design of locomotive, with one size for each specific duty, as opposed to the existing 'Big Four' designs, already doing the jobs for which they had been designed? New designs had to be phased in, scrapping one lot completely was not practical until the new designs were operational, so one had to be run down whilst the other was built up. This phasing-in/phasing-out approach doubled the 'spares' problems and all the while the same procedures continued – steam hauled, same speeds, same stock etc.!

Changes had been made with carriage construction with all-welded frames and bodies by the 1950s. In the world of carriages and wagons a 'one-design-fits-all' thought was gathering momentum. (See Appendix B for a note on the importance of welding in maintenance and construction.)

Radical new thinking saw steam being rapidly phased out – seemingly every company except the Great Western hopping onto the new diesel bandwagon! The Swindon trades unions insisting on building the last passenger-steam locomotive *Evening Star* whilst everyone else was tooling up for diesel production. With steam eventually gone, the 1960s saw great design changes in carriage and thus in train design: the Blue Pullmans – six or eight trains with a power car at each end – new interiors to coaches using plastic laminates, glass, installation of air brakes, eliminating the traditional vacuum, a series of 'marks' including a new carriage construction method substituting the separate underframe for a box structure which reduced weight. In the 1980s, further 'advancement' saw the British Rail carriages using a version of the Swiss 'Schlieren' bogie, which was apparently not as smooth running on our track as on the original Swiss.

The series of marks mentioned went from II in the early 1970s through the alphabet to F then on to Mark III. But all really too late for Swindon which in 1987 had lost not only its original C&W Works, but the complete Swindon Loco and Carriage & Wagon Works which no longer existed.

CARRIAGE BOGIE DESIGN *c.*1970

B.R. Standard
Bogie Mark II.

Modified
BR Standard
Bogie
Mark IIA,
incorporating
knife-edge
suspension.

CODES FOR VEHICLE TYPES CODE

BR Standard Passenger Vehicles	1
Former Regional Passenger Vehicles	2
Pullman Cars	3
Sleeping Cars	4
Non-Passenger Bogie	5
Non-Passenger Non-Bogie	6
Kitchen Cars	7
Other Catering Vehicles	8

METHOD AND EXAMPLES OF CODING VEHICLES

Upon receipt of vehicles into a Main Works the vehicle type code and agreed repair classification will be chalked on the underframe, in that order, with an oblique stroke (/) to separate the codes.

EXAMPLES

(a) A standard BR loco hauled passenger vehicle requiring a Class 3 repair will be written.   1/3

(b) A former regional passenger vehicle requiring a Class 4 repair will be written. 2/4

(c) A sleeping car requiring a Class 2 repair will be written.   4/2

(d) A non-passenger bogie vehicle requiring a Class 4 repair will be written.   5/4

(e) A catering vehicle requiring premature attention to the gas system will be written.   8/5

(f) A standard BR passenger vehicle having damage requiring a Class 2 repair will be written 1/2/D if cost of damage is required ½ Repair WO Damage

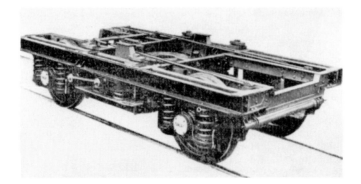

B4 bogie.

Commonwealth bogie.

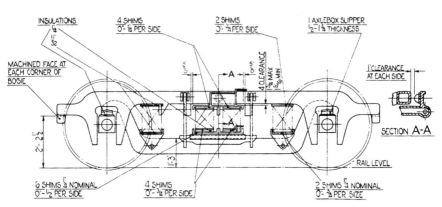

Diagram of Commonwealth bogie.

From this point onwards, it would be hard not to notice the difference in the carriage stock: reclining seats, air conditioning and double glazing. We could also mention time keeping, commuter crushes, and what about the cost of fares! To the ordinary passenger nowadays, however, carriages probably seem to function the same as always, but continue to cost more and more each time they travel!

WELDING OF PEDESTAL LINERS

1. Remove old horn guide liners by chipping off the weld and when the liners have been removed, any weld still attached to the pedestal must be cleaned up.

2. Set new liners against the pedestal leg at a height of ½in from the pedestal toe. By placing jacks between the two liners in one axle box opening. Ensure that the liners are a tight fit against the pedestal face and the inner side of the pedestal leg before welding. The liners applied to the outer pedestal leg should NOT have cut-outs for the equalisers.

3. Bogie frame should be set so all welds can be made without moving frame. Make three welds approximately 2in long on each edge of the liners. As indicated on liners with cut-outs for equalisers, place weld 2in long on both inner edges of cut-out, 1in down from the top. This latter weld must not reduce size of opening in pedestal for equaliser below 3 ⅝ in.

4. Use an electrode to British Standard 1719 code E306.

   All welds should be made with two beads. First, lay a thin vertical down bead on the pedestal leg adjacent to the liner. Direct the electrode towards the pedestal leg, flowing the weld metal to the liner edge, effecting weld metal attachment to the liner. Follow immediately with an overlaying up bead deposited in the same manner as the first. Use 10 gauge electrodes with amperage from 90 to 105. The use of indicated amperages and thin initial bead avoids excessive penetration and keeps temperature low. This protects the rubber bonding of the liners. Directing the electrode towards the pedestal and flowing weld metal to the liner edge, prevents excessive dilution of the weld metal by the liner material. These practices provide greatest insurance against cracking.

   The welding sequence described above, avoids stresses which would result in cracking and bowing of the liner material.

   The completed welds must be convex as shown in Fig. 2A and should readily result from up bead application.

   The minimum width of the connection to the casting to be the thickness of the liner.

   Complete one liner at a time.

   Let welds cool before removing jacks.

5. On pedestal legs where filler blocks are used, additional welds as shown in Fig. 3 are to be placed on bottom edge of liners to stiffen the pedestal legs.

   (a) Where the filler blocks have been removed, care must be taken when replacing them to ensure that the filler block rivet heads are not proud of the pedestal (i.e. the rivet heads must not obstruct the fixing of the pedestal liner).

6. Brakework: Repeat 1–4.

   Examine all components for condition and replace all bushes, pins or bolts having wear greater than ¹/₆₄in on the nominal diameter. Restore all unbushed holes to drawing dimensions. On re-assembly thoroughly grease all items with one of the following:

Grease	Manufacturer	BR Cat No.
Grippa 83	Castrol	9/27/3350
Mytilus B	Shell	9/27/4065
Cazar K1	Esso	9/27/2570

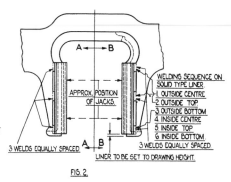

FIG. 2

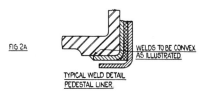

FIG 2A

TYPICAL WELD DETAIL
PEDESTAL LINER.

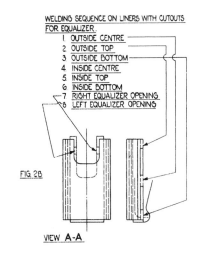

FIG. 2B

VIEW A-A

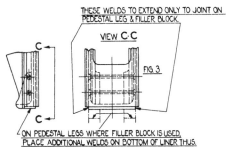

VIEW C-C

FIG. 3

EXAMPLES OF BOGIE DESIGNS

Bolster type with volute springs.

'American' type with coil springs.

Bolster type with coil springs.

Churchward's 'American' type.

GOODS TRAIN STOCK

Long before the railway-passenger carriage made its entry, the transport of other goods 'by rail' had made an appearance. We mentioned earlier the little four-wheeled wagons running first on boards, then on a sequence of better designed track, then from boards to strips of wood on to varying and improving shapes of rail of cast iron, through to wrought iron and eventually to steel.

These little wagons were designed to be pulled by the only available power sources – man and horse – and so were designed to suit. All that changed, however, when steam made its appearance. More power meant heavier loads, and so larger wagons evolved. The first little wagons or 'Chaldrons' were designed specifically for rail use, where the rail and wagon are of joint importance as one has to run smoothly on the other, and the wheel design is as equally significant, as it is permanently twinned and associated. The construction of the Chaldron was completely by hand as there were no machine tools. The main timber baulks were hand sawn by two men working with a double-handled saw over a saw pit, one man on top of the timber baulk and one in the pit under the baulk, the saw being used vertically – a very tough job even with sawyers to suit. (Sawyers had a reputation as heavy drinkers, probably to deaden the muscular pain of sawing!) Joints were mortise and tenon, the wood for the frame cut by adze, and the joints secured by wood dowels. Frames individually made using hand tools and reinforced by iron brackets made by a blacksmith and secured with smith-made iron nails.

Although shown here with the flanged wheels, this was a later development on the introduction of the 'edge rail'. The early Chaldrons ran on plateways from tram roads where the plates were flat with a raised side, not for running the wheels on top, but to keep them from running off the plate, as shown by the photos of larger and later versions. The very first wheels followed the designs of the road wagon, first as a solid-wood disc, later with spokes and centre bearing like a smaller road coach wheel, usually with a wrought-iron band or tyre. The capacity and weight to be carried varied with the load, from 1–3 tons. Some old illustrations show them with no form of brake, so loose-coupled trains could easily run away, even on a slight gradient, overtake and injure the horse, before running off the track and overturning!

As the tramways and plateways developed into railways, so the Chaldron design developed into larger and larger wagons, and with the designs developed a new trade status for those who built them and thus the 'wagon builder' became a specific job. As bigger and heavier wagons developed, their movement in linked columns, now a number towed by a steam locomotive, began to become difficult to manage and control. Towing was by either bar or chain and the only buffing arrangement to dampen the end-to-end contacts inevitable with moving columns

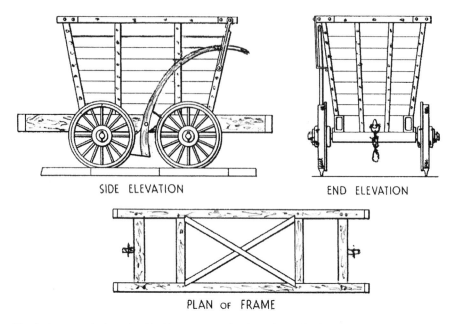

SIDE ELEVATION   END ELEVATION

PLAN of FRAME

The first wagon design: the Chaldron. Reputed to have been the first railway wagon with four wheels. The illustration is based on an old print, dated 1803. (The Chaldron is also an old measure of coal, equal to 36 bushels.)

of wagons were the extended solid ends of the two main frame lengths. Every builder had his own theories and measurements so a vast array of different designs emerged, which meant, as the railways began to be standardised, something had to be done about regulating measurements, and reducing the solid impacts of shunting the wagons. Incidentally, buffers on the Fire Fly Class locomotives of 1840 were stumpy leather cylinders, a couple of metal bands round them, and stuffed with horsehair.

Around the end of the 1870s, thoughts were turning to the use of springs to reduce and control the impacts of shunting wagons, assembling wagons quite heavily loaded as they increased in size. So, the makers, be it railway companies or private firms, set up a committee, calling itself The Railway Clearing House, to which it was proposed all makers submitted their designs for approval. Conforming to some standard agreed measurements ensured that the various makers' designs – the top 'bodies' of which could still vary greatly depending on the loads to be carried – had some secure method of coupling with the chassis frame and thus some shock-absorbing qualities. Then along came designs of standardised draw gear and buffing mechanism. Thus any combination of wagon

LATER DEVELOPMENTS FROM THE 'CHALDRON'

Wood-framed wagon with wheels like a road cart on a way. Wheels revolve on a fixed axle.

Riveted iron wagon for stone slate or coal with wood frame and wheels which revolved on a fixed frame. Separate cast-iron tramways.

A wood-framed and bodied tramway wagon. Iron bracket reinforced on wrought-iron fish-bellied tramway edge rail lengths. Wheels revolve on fixed axles. Note the iron band bound frame ends to act as 'buffers' and the flanged wheels to suit the edge rails.

designs had at least one section standardised so they could be all coupled to form a train and so developed the spring buffer, and the continuous draw gear at set positions on the wagon frame.

In 1887 the committee issued a specification to which all manufacturers had to conform, with an inspection to ensure they did. If verified, the committee issued two register plates, one each side of the wagon, proving that it had conformed to the 'spec.'.

The specification was comprehensive, standardising the sizes of wheels and axles: journals 3¾-in diameter x 8in long, wheels 3ft in diameter, although there could be variations of an inch or two. These were made with cast-iron centres with the spokes and rim cast-in, and were secured to the axles which themselves revolved within grease-filled axle boxes, the revolving 'wagon wheel' of the early years now abandoned. Sizes of wood for the various frame members were specified in oak, with a set wheelbase of 9ft and 5ft 8½in between buffer centres. Standardisation of the wood frame in 1887 was followed, really quite rapidly, by an upgrade to a similar structure plan, but this time in riveted steel, in 1889, and still retaining the leaf-spring buffer design. The length of the standard body design was 16ft 6in with a width of 8ft.

The Railway Clearing House was still controlling designs, which were to some extent allowed to vary as speeds and types of goods to be transported developed, but still retaining the basic structure. So the four-wheel wagon continued in use, and of the many thousands operating it was an impossible job to scrap one design in favour of another updated version, so it became essential to retain as many as possible but updated in the best way acceptable to the Railway Clearing House who still pulled the strings.

As we have seen, buffing and draw-gear improvements led to registering and plating in the usual way. The leaf spring had been superseded by the self-contained volute or coil spring and some wagons of very early date so altered, a number from before 1887, were still in traffic up to nationalisation; the updating and conversions continuing in tandem with new wagon construction up to the First World War.

In 1923 the Railway Clearing House issued a new specification form relating to wood-wagon frame construction for a 12-tonner. The specification included standard details for a steel frame, its steel structure of heavier gauge metal than the 1889 version. The wheel bearings were now to run in oil-axle boxes. Dictated by faster speeds of the trains, some wagons, for example coal and coke wagons, had axle boxes designed so that a much faster way of emptying them evolved, which did not rely on the usual operator with a shovel. These could be secured in a rotating fixture which turned the complete wagon upside down and the oil stayed where it should be. Grease-type boxes were replaced with oil boxes, which lubricated on movement and did not require a period to 'warm up' to make the lubricant flow. Oil-axle boxes were adopted generally in 1897.

Whilst the four-wheel wagon, irrespective of its use and body design was – as the classic saying goes – 'like the poor, always with us!', loads were changing in nature and bulk and some now had six wheels. There was a limit regarding the turning circle when the wheelbase is considered, particularly where wagons were carrying liquids in cylindrical tanks on a railway underframe, where, incidentally the tank was owned by the customer. Loads such as these continued to get longer and heavier, and double-bogie wagon types were ordered as early as 1948 – of which more later!

Approaching 1870 the broad-gauge mileage was at its greatest and the change-of-gauge problems accelerated. Standard-gauge four-wheelers continued to be built at Worcester and Saltney until 1874, but the new Works at Swindon had, in 1871 produced four 20-ton six-wheel open-goods wagons; they had a limited use but survived to about 1912 for special loads. With experience from his travels in South America, J. Wilkinson, the new chief goods manager, had built, as an experiment in 1888, a 25-ton open-goods wagon on double four-wheel bogies. Unfortunately, it appeared several years before its time, as it was only ever able to get half-capacity loads during the twelve-month period in which it was trialled. These loads could have been carried in the standard wagon of 10 tons, so bigger vehicles had to wait a decade. Wagons of 20 tons were specially introduced in 1897 for the transport of its own locomotive coal over the Great Western system, rising to 40-ton wagons in 1905. These constructions were all steel. It apparently took another two decades to persuade the private owners to use these 20-tonners!

An event detailed earlier in this book was the introduction in 1903 of the vacuum brake to goods vehicle stock. Big double-bogie vehicles were now being introduced for the larger special loads (one later example is illustrated on page 79 out of the dozens which were developed). Routine batches of bogie wagons for such goods as motorcars, locomotive boilers, military vehicles, large guns, battle tanks etc. were built in considerable numbers. Ordinary goods van specials now included refrigerator vans and steam-heated banana vans.

Even the double-bogie wagons had their own 'specials' to carry armour plate, ships propellers, steel coils and bars or tubes. There were even 'special specials' including a 135-ton transformer wagon 89ft long, each end supporting a giant central girder: the whole on six-wheel bogies, two each end, making twenty-four wheels. Also there were the real specials to carry nuclear waste! The Swindon Works C&W Department was involved in making a batch of specials in the 1950s but the 'writing was on the wall' with talk of closure of the Works.

In the years following the closure of the sites housing Swindon's C&W Works, and the transfer of a fraction of it to the fast emptying locomotive workshops, the vacuum braking systems were being replaced by the more effective air brakes, and much of the work of the C&W Works was being transferred elsewhere. There was also a move to utilise redundant carriage and underframes for virtually palletised loads in the form of four covered goods body-style containers along the length of the underframe, giving a look of the later 'containerisation' transport. The Great Western made use of 144 such underframes. A number were fitted with Westinghouse air-brake pipework for full Westinghouse application. 1948 saw the

RAILWAY WAGONS

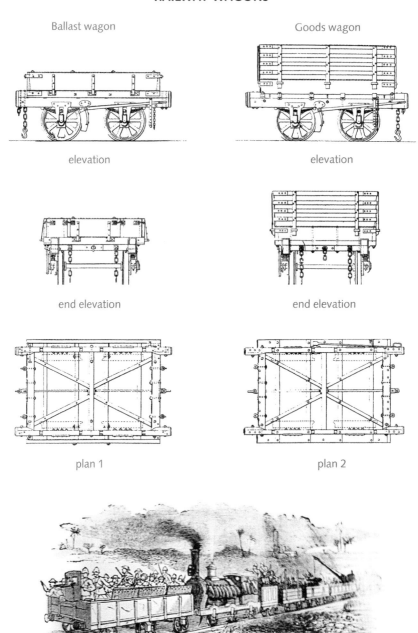

Ballast wagon

elevation

end elevation

plan 1

Goods wagon

elevation

end elevation

plan 2

British iron-clad train in Egypt: another use for the railway wagon, *c.* 1870. There seemed to be a flush of 'armoured train' designs in the late 1800s. The enemy had only to take out a track section to render the whole train useless!

STANDARD WAGON CHASSIS DESIGNS

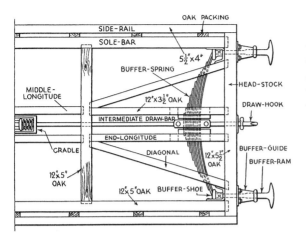

1887 specification spring buffer, which show very few changes over a period from 1887–1923 apart from changing the material from wood to iron to steel. Note the single 'leaf spring' for buffers.

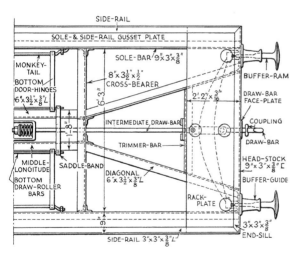

1889 steel or iron underframe. The 'leaf' spring, which may seem a rather cumbersome arrangement, lasted in use until about 1900 when it was replaced by a volute spring in a self-contained buffer. This was later changed for the simple coil spring arrangement shown below.

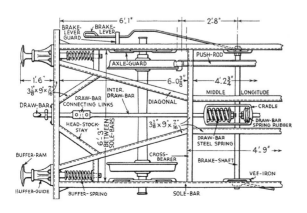

1923 arrangement of standard 13-ton steel wagon frame.

EXAMPLE WAGON DIAGRAMS FROM THE 1850S

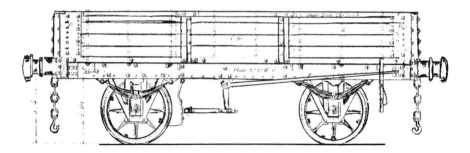

Open goods wagon, the design of which did not change over the following years. Vacuum and air brakes added much later, but still recognisable on preserved heritage railways today.

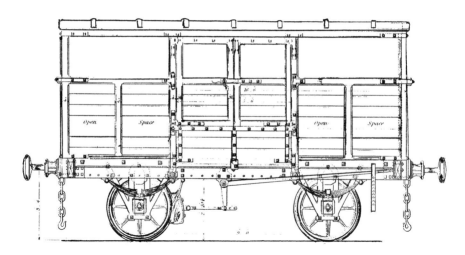

Cattle wagon: note the large wood brake blocks later cast iron but still operated in the same way by the hand lever. Wood underframes changed to iron and steel over the years but the bodies were still made of wood.

introduction of containers for use on single wagons. The 1949 wagon-building programme had Swindon altering the 8-ton weight designation of a cattle wagon, a design virtually years old, now changed to 12 tons almost identical to the early versions in the body design. Most special wagons had 2ft 8½in-diameter wheels as used on examples constructed at Swindon; a batch of forty-two were of the 12-ton 'glass truck'. Although of LMS-design origin, ideas, designs and construction were now Nationalised, and spread to any available and suitable workshop.

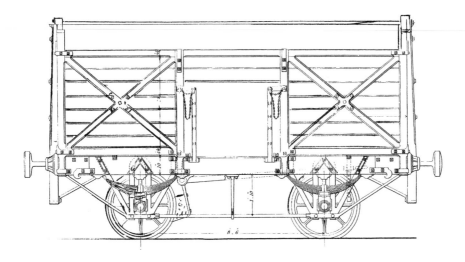

Coke wagon: the design of the wheels changed over the years to rolled steel discs. Wood underframes changed for new wagons over the years to iron and steel, but wood bodies remained in use.

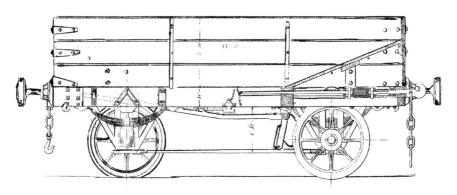

Coal wagon: standard continuous-draw gear introduced, later with self-contained buffers.

During the Second World War, the No. 7 Finishing Shop had two-man submarine components on its list. Invasion barges were built in the Wagon Shops and No. 24 Shop, the large carriage shop, was taken over by the Ministry of Defence for the construction of Stirling Bomber parts, wings etc. under the watchful eye of Short Brothers.

From the early 1950s the work continued to diminish, until the C&W Works appeared in a much-reduced form, into the also diminishing Locomotive Works. By 1987, the Loco, Carriage & Wagon had gone completely. The Swindon Works no longer existed.

Below is the 20-ton coal wagon which the Great Western Railway hoped to persuade the coal owners to use instead of the smaller 10-ton, usual version. A train of 20-tonners was about 40 per cent shorter in length than a train of the 10-tonners for the same weight of coal transported.

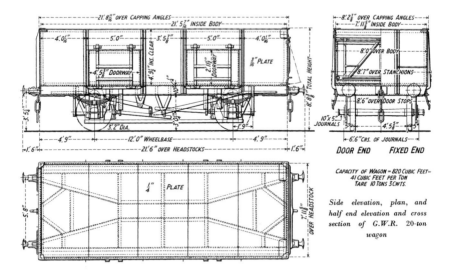

20-ton coal wagon. One thousand 20-tonners were ordered from four private manufacturers, the wagons of all metal construction and 250 wagons were ordered from each of the following companies: Gloucester Carriage & Wagon Co. Ltd; Birmingham Railway Carriage & Wagon Co. Ltd; Bute Works Supply & Co. Ltd; Stableford & Co. Ltd.

Swindon C&W Works had an order for 200 20-tonners, whilst the Loco Works received an order for a suitable new tank locomotive with 0-6-2 wheel arrangement to accompany the new coal wagons. A first order for fifty started the ball rolling toward updating transport for the coal industry, a final total of 200 completing the 'new look'.

16-ton all-steel welded frame (mineral wagon), 1946.

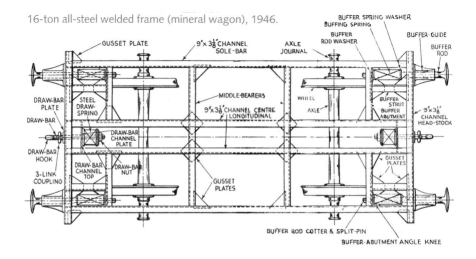

As railways and what they were expected to carry continued to develop into the twentieth century, the 'special' wagons proliferated. Long designs with the usual four wheels developed alongside the 'bogie' versions. The specials had a 'diagram book', not to be included with the lesser mortals for general, sheep, pigs, cattle etc. transport. There were many variations and 'marks', the above example is just one of dozens to show general design features of the range.

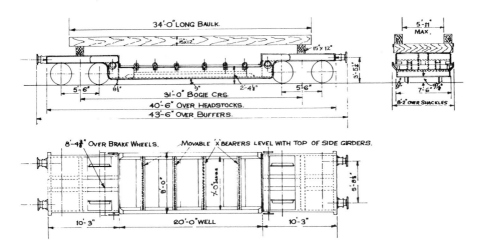

25-ton 'well wagon': there were two types of 25-ton bogie well wagons lettered 'Weltrol'.

Riveting of iron 'A' steel frames was to be overtaken by the development of gas and electric arc welding, thus introducing a new 'trade' classification to all constructors in the field of engineering. The layout is recognisable from their wood frame forebears. Note also through the centre length the continuous draw gear linking the drag hooks on both ends of the wagon. You can just make out the historical hand brake lever in the middle frame on the right-hand side.

LATER (1920S–30S) WAGON DESIGNS: FRUIT VAN, FISH VAN AND CATTLE VAN.

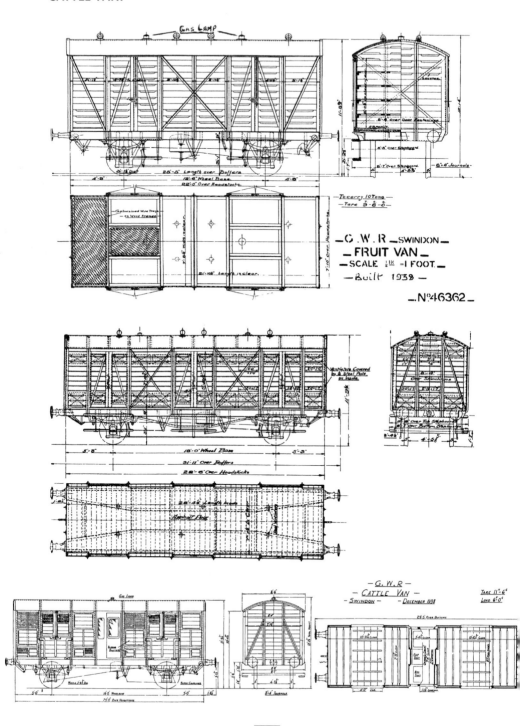

SPECIAL USE WAGONS – RAILWAY BREAKDOWN TRAINS 1880–1950

What future awaits this section of steam cranes at the end of the steam era? In front with its jib down on its match truck is a Cowans Sheldon Special, built in 1941, for the Engineering Department, capacity 12 tons at 15ft radius. Immediately behind is a 75-tonner with an auxiliary hoist of 12 tons, acquired by British Rail in 1961. Third is the circular holed jib of a standard Great Western permanent-way crane with a capacity of 6 tons at 15ft radius. The rear example is a Ransome & Rapier of 45 tons' capacity, built in 1940.

Among the specialist wagon designs was the 'Match Truck', which carried the lowered crane jib for transport as well as wood baulks and tools, for work on breakdowns and crashes.

Part of the inevitable crash site paperwork.

GREAT WESTERN RAILWAY.

LOCOMOTIVE AND CARRIAGE DEPARTMENT.

....Station. ....190...

REPORT OF OPERATIONS OF BREAK-DOWN GANG.

Date of Accident ....190......
Time ,, ,, ...
Site ,, ,, ...
Time Message received at Shed ....
,, Vans left Shed ....
,, ,, ,, Station ....
,, ,, arrived at site ....
,, Break-down Gang commenced work ....
,, ,, ,, finished ,, ...
,, Vans left site of Accident ....
,, ,, arrived at Shed...
Description of Lines blocked..
....
Time Lines cleared ....
....
Single Line working from (time) ....to (time)...
No. of Men in Break-down Gang ....
Description of B.D. Crane ....
Work done with Crane ....
  REMARKS.—Give particulars, if Crane available, but not used—probable cause of Accident, &c.
NOTE.—This Report must be sent to the Divisional Loco. Superintendent's Office immediately on return of the vans, and to be followed at the earliest possible moment by a complete report giving full details of damage to stock and cost of clearing the line.

VARIOUS WAGON COMPONENTS:
note the pressed bogie frame below. Others were fabricated from steel channel and angle, riveted or welded, or cast in steel.

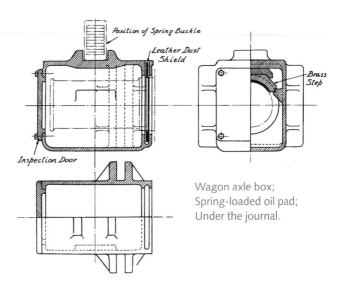

Wagon axle box;
Spring-loaded oil pad;
Under the journal.

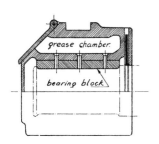

Wagon axle box (grease lubrication).

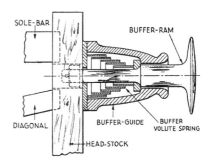

Self-contained spring buffer.

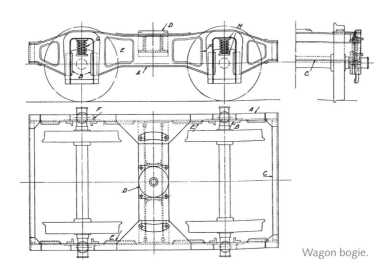

Wagon bogie.

WHEEL AND AXLE DESIGN FROM THE EARLY YEARS

In the late nineteenth century there were two major questions being discussed: one question was over the ideal wheel diameter. The other was regarding the placement of the wheels – should they be under or outside the coach body, the latter method apparently already tried and abandoned by the Great Western in their dabble with the 'posting carriage' design, and with large-diameter wheels outside proving inconvenient. We take it for granted now that all railway transport has wheels solidly fixed and keyed to axles in which the complete set revolves the bearing seats on the axles. But back then it caused much debate. On going around a curve the outside wheel had more distance to travel than the one on the inside, therefore it must drag and slip to a certain extent. As in a road vehicle design, the wheel revolved on a fixed axle so that a 'differential velocity' was obtained.

In D. Clark's analysis of carriage and wagon wheel design (1854) he quotes Adam's design. He advocated an iron-disc wheel with a chilled cast-iron tyre. In this design, the wheel is free to turn on the axle, which is also free to rotate in

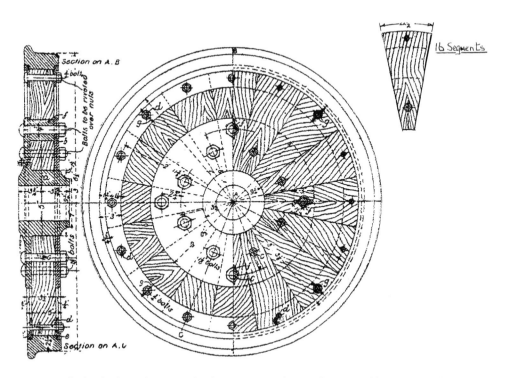

Mansell wheel, 3ft 5in diameter: this design was used over a long period by most British railway companies.

its grease-lubricated axle box. How the wheel itself is lubricated is not specified. The design of the axle is also discussed at length. There must be no sharp corners in the design and there must be smooth, tapered contours when an increase or reduction in diameter is required, even to the extent of tapered journals for the bearing surfaces. The question of hollow axles was also raised, as in such designs introduced by the 'Patent Shaft & Axle Tree Company', where a benefit of weight reduction is emphasised, as is strength equal to the solid version. Clark concludes: 'we must, one day, arrive at loose wheels turning independently on axles; and then there will be no more torsion, when there will cease to be any practical advantage in the hollow over the solid axle.' Arguments still raged over grease or oil lubrication. Fitting a grease drawer in the bottom of the box was tried and rejected as troublesome, 'but an oil pad in the box, as used in America, is said to be working well and economically in England.' The fixed wheel-axle combination still remains! So the design for revolving wheels on fixed or revolving axles died a natural death.

There were great variations in carriage and wagon wheel designs in the early years: cast iron, blacksmith-made wrought iron, cast-iron centres with spokes and rims of wrought iron 'cast-in'. After the work of Henry Bessemer, cast steel wheels generally became the norm for the locomotives wheels of around 6ft diameter, the 'wheel set' complete with axles with crank webs became common. Development led to the solid rolled disc wheel, in the smaller carriage and wagon requirement sizes in diameters of around 3ft, in some instances rolled complete with the flange profile (which was usually provided by means of a separate tyre, shrunk on and retained additionally by a 'ring' fixing). In this way a worn solid wheel could be machined to take a separate tyre. There were several designs of this ring fixing, but one was to take over on the Great Western to accommodate a specific design of carriage wheel. Whilst the usual design of ring was rolled to seal, the 'Mansell' design was bolted through the wood block centre. This experiment proved successful and was to be applied to the Great Western carriage stock, utilising the damping down for quieter running wheels. This design of wood sections to form the wheel centre was eventually superseded by the usual spoked or disc wheel, its tyre secured by a 'Gibson' ring. The thousands of shaped wood Mansell blocks were thus redundant and were used as floor blocks in many of Swindon's workshops. (It's much easier on the feet of the various tradesmen, for example standing all day before a lathe in one of the Machine Shops, than it would be on the usual concrete floor.)

The wheel tyre has had a long existence. Used on the wooden wheels of road transport not to hold the wood wheel together but to reduce wear damage, it was applied in strips or strakes, each strake bolted through the wheel rim, which itself was in sections, over the joints. The shrunk-on ring tyre is a later development, e.g. to gun carriages in the 1860s.

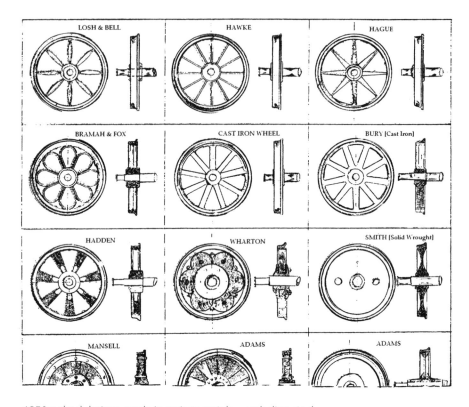

1850s wheel designs, made in various metals – excluding steel.

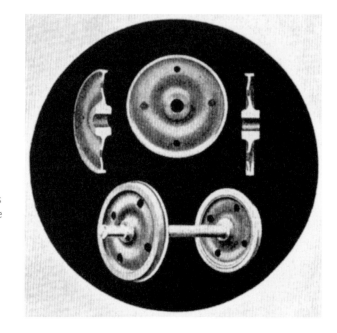

'Empire brand' rolled-steel disc wheels – a wheel-set complete with tyres and secured to the axle. By 1900, wheels with cast-iron centres were not allowed. (Courtesy of Messrs Taylor Bros & Co. Ltd)

The 1850s smith-made railway wheel had the usual wrought-iron ring tyre, and Brunel was very concerned about the rapid wear experienced. In an attempt to reduce this problem, which was successful, he instructed that a steel bar should be rolled into the iron tyre. With the heating to shrink on the tyre, the cooling and 'work hardening' of rolling it was found that the carbon steel lathe tools made by the blacksmith could not cope with the profile machining of the tyre, which, to modern eyes would not have been a problem, but was now too hard.

The alternative was thus grinding and that is a tale by itself. At that period, there were no grinding wheels as we know them today! No composite structures to include special abrasives to suit the material requirement. The grindstones of the period were of necessity natural stone shaped into a circular format, which was a most difficult procedure, leaving a finished stone with built-in killer potential! Any flaw in the stone, hidden in the depths of some of the big stones could, and did, cause a stone to explode whilst in use and could decapitate the operator! We don't realise how lucky we now are using a grindstone. So, as well as the lathe, there was now an additional operation in the manufacture of a wheel and an additional machinery requirement.

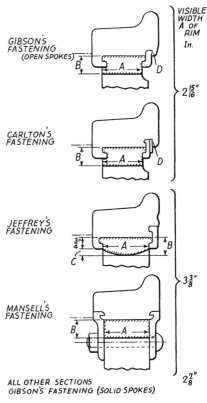

METHODS OF FASTENING THE TIRE

Methods of fastening the tyre: although the tyre was heated to expand it, and was allowed to shrink onto the wheel, it was still further secured by special 'locking rings' of various designs all with a single purpose, to ensure it stayed on. As the tyre wore it could be machined once or twice down to a limit, then it was removed and replaced by a new tyre.

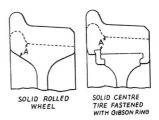

A standard 'craven' 4ft 0in faceplate wheel lathe. (Courtesy of C.B. Collet, Esq. OBE, Chief Mechanical Engineer, Great Western Railway Co., Swindon Shops)

A typical example of general wagon suspension for four- or six-wheel designs. The rolled steel three-hole wheel and the oil axle box, topped up by lifting the small spring flap, bottom centre of the axle-box keep containing the journal-lubricating pad.

The effect of 'work hardening' on wheel tyres is a continuing problem. The 'hammer' blow over the rail joints, lessening as the effect of the later introduction of the 'long welded rail' eliminated at least a portion of the events, added to the friction and close contact of the rail and rolling surface of the tyre. Couple all of these events to the friction of the application of the brakes, the heating and cooling of the tyre surface, and a glass-like finish was obtained on the tyre in addition to the normal wear and tear.

The development of the 'wheel lathe' (see page 88) is capable of all of the machining operations on railway stock wheels. The lathe cutting tools which developed to replace the carbon steel efforts of the blacksmith now included the much harder carbide-tipped tools which, whilst they could get under the work hardening layer, the facility of grinding built into the design of the wheel lathe ensured economy in the removal of metal, thus extending the life of the wheel set.

With this grinding facility a complete wheel-set machining process could include 'cleaning up' the journals, without excessive metal removal, and with the method of the period of white metalled phosphor bronze half bearings, economy was again ensured. The modern use of ball and roller bearings in the modernising of the bearings has just added expense to replace bearings which worked effectively anyway since the early years of the railways.

4

THE RISE OF THE CRAFT WORKFORCE

The craftsman, be it engineering or woodworking, developed skills in tandem with the developing railways. The need for increasing precision in the making of metal and wooden components honed the skills of those tackling such work for the first time, and setting new standards of finish to the components made. Passing these skills on to new recruits, the skilled Guild members, themselves having to learn new skills, set the standards to be passed on to those following. Thus the master craftsmen had to ensure those who followed were properly instructed.

The principle of established apprenticeships was accepted very early on by the Great Western Railway (GWR), and even here, later circumstances devised a form of elitist acceptance and grouping. The fitter and turner and locomotive erecting trades became accepted as first-class trades, all other engineering trades being looked on as second-class. Due to the numbers of employees involved (Swindon alone in its heyday employed about 13,500), there was never a shortage of applicants for any of the many trades which were practised within the GWR area and so great were the number of applicants that a system of selection evolved and was indeed essential. The trades themselves were evolving and developing, an example being wagon and carriage building. From the early rough 'Chaldron' wagon to the iron double-bogie bolster versions, over a forty-year period, the carriages getting bigger and more elaborate as well.

With fishing or mining, for example, often son followed father into the boat or down the pit, the son of the railway employee followed the same course, with the usual complication of the larger families at that time, and the trades to be followed getting more sophisticated with each generation. There were also limitations to the number of apprenticeships granted per family. The father being, say a first-class trade fitter and turner could obtain apprenticeships for only the first two sons in a first-class trade. Subsequent family applicants from the larger families of those days could obtain only second-class trades. Thus my father became a boilermaker, whilst his two elder brothers became fitters (both incidentally left the Works to take up supervision positions on the Indian railways, one on the East India Railway and one on the Madras & Southern Mahratta).

If a first-class trade vacancy was available for apprenticeship, a second-class tradesman could actually purchase such an apprenticeship for his son. The cost was £100 in the 1940s, a considerable sum at that time. This cost was abolished on nationalisation of the railways in 1947. A further special apprenticeship was that of 'student' or 'pupil', when a lad from outside the sphere of the railway would start a specialist course through the shops, often as part of a university study course. Destined to become a professional engineer in due course, not necessarily with the railway, these apprentices were introduced to management, drawing office and administration during the selected employment period. They would be carefully shepherded through the special period in the workshops, not following the complete course of ordinary apprentices but, instead, learning about specialist management functions.

Early training for all apprentices was the strictly practical, sequenced moves through the workshops themselves. The fitters and turners had several relevant shops at their disposal but some Carriage & Wagon Works trades were restricted to the shops undertaking specific duties. There was no apprentice school of any sort until much later, and then almost too late, but effective for a time. It should also be understood that, for example at Swindon Works, the number of apprentices, for all trades, was far more than would have been required for maintaining the manning of the Works. Assistance with production was the return the company received for the training given. When the five years had elapsed, usually at the age of 21, the apprentice received his indentures along with the dismissal notice! His training now over, it was then up to him to take his skills elsewhere, to improve by practice, becoming the 'journeyman' of old. Several times war interrupted an apprenticeship. Page 97 shows an official form covering such interruption for service in the Second World War, the period of apprenticeship being completed officially on return. A similar scheme applied in the First World War, and later for National Service. With the latter, the dismissal notice became irrelevant as call-up immediately on completion of apprenticeship followed. One year's employment was guaranteed on return then dismissal if unlucky! If the job was deemed permanent, as in my experience, work continued.

During the apprenticeship, practical knowledge was gained by working on the production machines and on the fitting benches actually repairing or producing locomotive and carriage and wagon components. Moves from shop to shop within the Works were possible, dependant on the trade, and gave a varied experience of varied jobs, each with its own characters who were the permanent residents doing those particular jobs. The apprentice worked with the tradesman, who was not a teacher as such, and generally picked up the working practices by actually doing them under supervision. Once experienced in a particular aspect of the work, the remaining period of a few weeks on the job contributed toward production, a return to the company for the trade teaching. Actually doing the work of the trade was really the only way of understanding the requirements.

The continued development of the companies involved in the amalgamations of 1921, which had seen the establishment of the four main groupings, had meant further expansion, in some cases, of the facilities of the absorbed companies. In this respect with Great Western absorptions, apprenticeships included a period seconded from smaller absorbed works and sheds to Swindon Works, with its wider array of operations. This gave seconded apprentices an additional experience in the construction of new locomotives, carriages and wagons – a process confined, during the period from the early 1900s onwards, to Swindon Works.

As an apprentice, I remember lads from South Africa and India also 'going the rounds' of the internationally accepted apprenticeship at Swindon Works – the apprentices returning to their homeland on completion; most of these lads with pupil or special status.

The theoretical, as well as the practical, side of the work was also catered for from quite early in the development of the GWR. There was from the earliest times a 'mutual improvement' interest among many exponents of the various trades employed.

As early as 1843, virtually as the new Works at Swindon settled down to production, a group library was formed at Swindon by a few members of the workforce. This intellectual approach was noticeable at other railway centres in the country and stemmed from trade growth and a desire to learn.

These self-stimulated groups were encouraged and supported by management and an embryo 'Mechanics Institution' was formed at Swindon within the Works itself, using a spare area above one of the workshops. The success of this venture led within ten years to the building of a separate 'Mechanics Institute' on land immediately opposite the main tunnel entrance to the Works. Study was encouraged and various lectures and musical events were arranged. The library was expanded continually, and was for many years the only library in Swindon. Later, non-railway employees could join, as well as a facility which allowed certain school seniors a visit every two weeks (I benefitted from the latter).

The number of students attending various classes held at the Institute continued to increase to such an extent, as the Works itself expanded, that by the end of the 1890s a new technical college was in existence under county, not railway control. Selected students were later allowed a 'day release' on full pay to attend the technical classes related to their trade. Others were required to attend the related classes in the evenings after the working day. This, of course, as with working life itself, appealed to some and not others, and attendances being notified back to the employer, as an unwritten condition of apprenticeship, explanations for non-attendance were to be proffered to the management.

Often staffed by Great Western employees, for example from the drawing office, the classes were concerned with the work actually undertaken. This could include the fitting and machining aspect, which could be applied to any mechanical situation, as well as the specific railway trades of carriage and wagon construction. Such classes were held at most centres of railway activity, not only at Swindon and the Great Western.

Such specialist trades were accepted and embraced by the Royal Society of Arts and City & Guilds of London Institute, and certificated by them. Thus those attending the courses and being successful in the examinations could obtain a certificate for their often specialist trade following. There were courses for railway coach & wagon carpentry, pattern making, road wagon building, steam boiler operators, boiler making, and foundry work, and so on. Opportunities were there for the taking for the interested apprentice or anyone wishing to gain specific knowledge. There were also the professional institutions to which aspiring professional engineers could belong. Admission was by election or, later, by set examinations, and all, as with the Guilds and Unions, had the protection of the members trade or professional status as a basic principle.

The civil engineers had formed their society or institution and received its charter in 1818, and, as technology developed, other splinter-group specialists formed other branches or separate groups. This included the mechanical engineer group and an electrical group was to follow, as this communication science developed in 1871. The moves toward standardisation in components and manufacture techniques were becoming essential, such requirements growing during the late nineteenth century, and in 1901 the Engineering Standards Committee was founded, which became what we now know as the BSI or British Standards Institution.

In Britain, up until the 1820s, the academic approach to practical engineering did not really exist, the subject being taught only on a trade basis. On the Continent, a different state of affairs existed. France had established the École Nationale des Ponts et Chaussées in 1747 (the oldest civil engineering university of the world), and the École Polytechnique in 1794. Germany established the Bauakademie in 1799, other schools following soon after, usually set up with government support.

In Britain, University College started a course of mechanical philosophy, followed eleven years later, in 1838, by King's College which commenced courses in civil engineering. Scotland followed suit in 1840 with courses established at Glasgow, all-in-all very late starters when compared to others in Europe, with a late move to 'examinations to determine membership suitability'.

Advances in technology, whilst originally spawning the splinter institutions of specialist disciplines, have, in latter years, drawn the specialist groups closer together. Thus was formed the Council of Engineering Institutions (CEI), an incorporation of fourteen chartered organisations of a specialist nature, now enabled, when occasion requires, of speaking with one voice, giving greater authority overall.

Following railway nationalisation in 1948, cash awards were made to all who were successful in the examinations of both City & Guilds and National Certificate examinations. It is fitting that the Guild's approach is still remembered, and associated with craft skills, in the title of the examination body itself.

A Great Western apprenticeship indenture was the passport to work all over the world, a railway training for a craft skill accepted as the 'top'. The apprenticeship document itself, the indenture, was, in the later years, a rather undistinguished paper. The early indentures were in the form of a legal document, setting out in clear detail the clauses and requirements by which all signing parties would be governed once the agreement of apprenticeship had been initiated. There was often an impressive seal attached, and the lengthy wording would be in the legal jargon of the period.

By the beginning of the twentieth century, the training given at, or under, the control of the major companies such as the GWR, was well known worldwide. All of the legal jargon on the original documents was now dropped as being rather dated and irrelevant. Many of the clauses and requirements were covered by the company rulebooks – a copy issued to each new entrant – and transgressions would be dealt with accordingly.

The indenture was still a major factor in the field of promotion to the supervisory staff. During the Second World War, with many craftsmen going into the armed forces, staff shortages meant that in some circumstances, for example, a 'fitters mate' was given a higher grade as an 'improver' or 'dilutee' standing in for a fully qualified fitter's post.

Many operators in the workshops had long memories, one of which comes to mind. Long after the war had ended and diesel had taken the place of steam, a promotion of an individual as a shop inspector triggered the recollection that he had been a 'dilutee' from a 'fitter's mate'. There was apparently no question that he was suitable for such a promotion, but he had not received the indenture for the trade, and was therefore not acceptable to the trade union concerned in a staff position as inspector. Fairness and trade knowledge were recognised, and many foremen and supervisors were respected and liked for such qualities, although some operators have always, since time began, resented discipline of any sort!

Restrictive practices, governing a particular trade regarding demarcation and like disputes, are being removed rapidly. Are we returning to a stage where a second-class tradesman in the millwrighting 'odd job' man capacity is once more emerging – someone with a smattering of a number of jobs but no actual trade as such? Time will tell, but the skilled hand craftsman is still a classification to be desired and achieved, particularly one who could teach and pass such practices on. Where will they be found in the future?

It was in the handling of components that trade demarcations arose. An example as late as the 1950s would be the introduction into the Carriage & Wagon Works of the high-speed copy lathes, used for axle turning. Once the stops and template had been installed, by a trained craftsman, virtually anybody could use the lathe, as cutting then became a high speed, tipped tool semi-automatic process. Should a craftsman or non craftsman use the machine? Some copy lathes stood idle for two years whilst this union/management dispute smouldered on! Robots, computer and tape controlled machines are now the norm! Where stands the original concept of the craftsman?

In the early years of the Great Western, many applications for engine driver positions came from trained engineers, and the 1846 regulations of the company included the provision, not only following the tradition that drivers also did locomotive running repairs, but that spare drivers should help the fitters in locomotive maintenance. This natural acceptance of relaxed demarcation of work was not to endure, and later adherence to strict guidelines was insisted upon. With the change from steam to diesel the structural work on the engine power unit bodies complicated the trade demarcation problems, who could weld what etc. Thus, from the early years, the specialist skills, or some of them, such as carriage and wagon building, coach finishing, carriage trimming, road wagon building and coach painting had now gone or at best changed beyond recognition, as had the Carriage & Wagon Works itself, back in the 1960s. By 1987 the entire Works had followed suit and closed completely.

The boilermakers, once so much in evidence, became platers and fabricators. No one wanted steam locomotive boilers anymore. The only boiler work as such left was that of the small train heating systems. There was not much call for cast iron items on a diesel locomotive, so faded the iron foundry pattern maker along with the Iron Foundry itself, the building at Swindon converted to a Diesel Engine Repair Shop (now part of a shopping mall – the Pattern Shop & Store building now a restaurant!) Heavy forging and drop hammer work became almost non-existent, so the big stamping shops were demolished both on the locomotive side as well as on the carriage and wagon. The Rolling Mill had already suffered the same fate. The Non Ferrous Brass & Aluminium Foundry was refurbished for a lengthened life, but with the departure of the steam locomotive, the whole system was dying.

Conversions were made over the region here and there for diesel locomotives and multiple units. Craftsmen trained on the steam locos also converting, reluctantly, to the glorified car mechanic's job of the diesel-engined locomotive.

One by one the Works were abandoned and most demolished. Wolverhampton, Caerphilly, Newton Abbott, and so on through to Swindon itself. The many thousands of craftsmen who had trained within their walls were now spread around the country and the world, the steam orientated crafts which are so proudly detailed on the apprenticeship indentures will die with the craftsmen themselves.

The steam-era locomotive, carriage and wagon men are now getting on in years, and a number are passing on their knowledge to amateur enthusiasts who

3

Great Western Railway.

Locomotive, Carriage & Wagon Department,

CHIEF MECHANICAL ENGINEER'S OFFICE.

C. B. COLLETT,
Chief Mechanical Engineer.

WHW

Swindon, Wilts, 21st. December 19 23.

Certificate of Training.

I hereby certify that

DENNIS HERBERT

born on the 29th. November 1901 *has been*

employed as a Machinist *in this Department*

as follows :-

Period of Training Five *years.*

from 29-11-1918 *to* 28-11-1923

Where employed Carriage Works, Swindon.

Work upon which engaged Drilling,Boring &Slotting
Machines.

HERBERT bears a good character, possesses

good ability as a workman, and has conducted

himself in a satisfactory manner.

CHIEF MECHANICAL ENGINEER.

G. W. R., Loco., Carriage and Wagon Department.

Certificate signed by C. Collett (1923) – trade: Machinist, Swindon. Carriage & Wagon Works example of Machine Shop work.

are following a very different form of unofficial apprenticeship. There will be no detailed GWR indenture for them, no matter how long they continue to do the job. The remaining steam locomotives, carriages and wagons now preserved on heritage railways still receiving attention from enthusiasts.

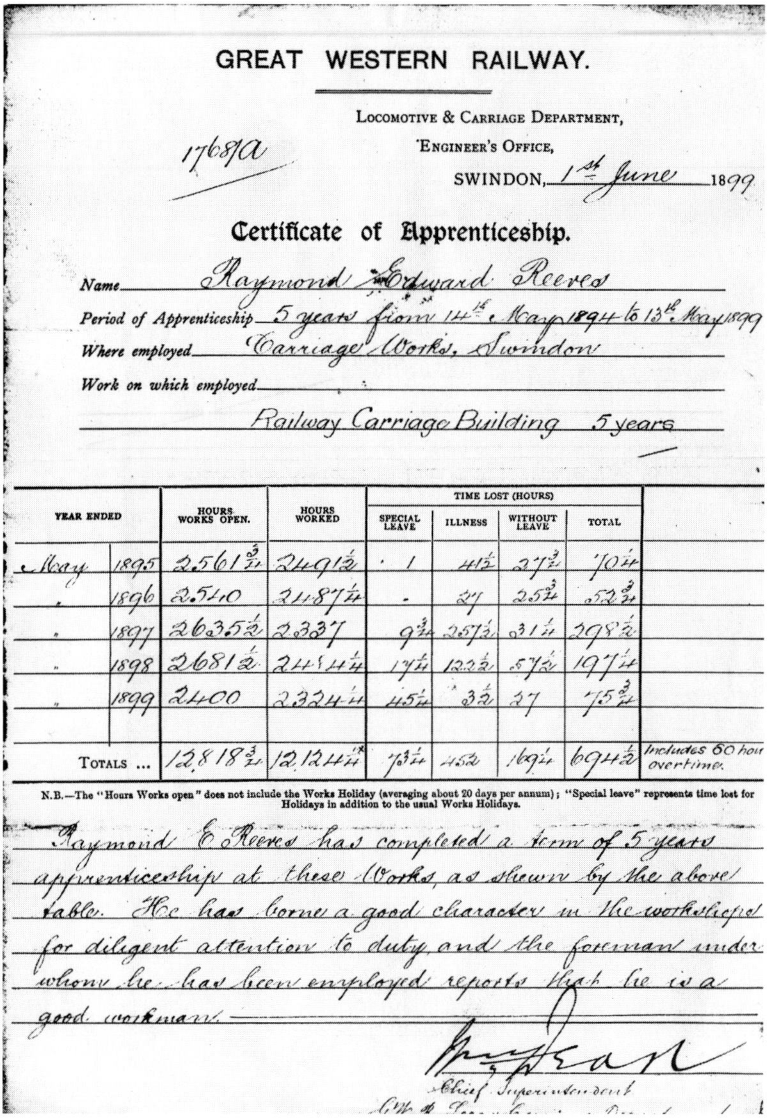

GREAT WESTERN RAILWAY.

LOCOMOTIVE & CARRIAGE DEPARTMENT,
ENGINEER'S OFFICE,

17687a

SWINDON, 1st June 1899

Certificate of Apprenticeship.

Name Raymond Edward Reeves

Period of Apprenticeship 5 years from 14th May 1894 to 13th May 1899

Where employed Carriage Works, Swindon

Work on which employed

Railway Carriage Building 5 years

YEAR ENDED		HOURS WORKS OPEN.	HOURS WORKED	TIME LOST (HOURS)				
				SPECIAL LEAVE	ILLNESS	WITHOUT LEAVE	TOTAL	
May	1895	2561¾	2491½	1	41½	27¾	70¼	
"	1896	2540	2187¼	-	27	25¾	52¾	
"	1897	2635½	2337	9¾	257½	31¼	298½	
"	1898	2681½	2484¼	17¼	122½	57½	197¼	
"	1899	2400	2324¼	45¼	3½	27	75¾	
TOTALS ...		12,818¾	12,124¼*	73¼	452	169¼	694½	*Includes 60 hou[rs] overtime.

N.B.—The "Hours Works open" does not include the Works Holiday (averaging about 20 days per annum); "Special leave" represents time lost for Holidays in addition to the usual Works Holidays.

Raymond E Reeves has completed a term of 5 years apprenticeship at these Works, as shewn by the above table. He has borne a good character in the workshops for diligent attention to duty, and the foreman under whom he has been employed reports that he is a good workman.

Wm Dean
Chief Superintendent

Certificate signed by William Dean, 1899 – trade: Railway Carriage Building, Swindon. Note how the format has changed from a legal document appearance to a record of work done and list of attendance hours.

It is hoped they will continue to keep 'steam' in all its aspects running for as long as possible, to maintain a long tradition of craft skills, and to keep the memory of all who have gone before.

Draft

BRITISH RAILWAYS BOARD

TRAINING CERTIFICATE

Certificate presented to the last decade of apprentices trained at Swindon Works (1983).

This Certificate records that

DAVID JOHN GALLAGHER

born 5TH March 1963 has been trained as

an Electrical Fitter

from 28th August 1979 to 23rd May 1983

Record of practical training and experience :

12 months Basic Craft Engineering Practices

24 months Engineering Industry Training Board Modules

JO1 - Mechanical Maintenance and JO2 Electrical Maintenance

on Rail Traction - Rolling Stock and Plant Maintenance

9 months applied electrical Traction and Rolling Stock experience

Record of further education :

City and Guilds - Craft Engineer...

City and Guilds - Craft Engineer...

City and Guilds Electrical Craft St...

City and Guilds Electrical Craft S...

Signed

(

for Br...

BR 9211

Corres. 7286/A.

SWINDON, Thurs, 4th October 1928

1928

Certificate of Apprenticeship.

Name ___ DAVID JOHN WHATLEY

Period of Apprenticeship Five years from 25th September 1923.

Where employed ___ Carriage & Wagon Works, Swindon.

Work on which employed ___

General Fitting and Machine Shop

Turning	31 months
Fitting	29 "
TOTAL	60 "

YEAR ENDED. 1928		HOURS WORKS OPEN.	HOURS WORKED.	TIME LOST (HOURS.)				
				SPECIAL LEAVE.	ILLNESS.	WITHOUT LEAVE.	TOTAL.	
Sept.	1924	2,302	2,313*	-	-	-	-	* Includes 11 hours overtime.
"	1925	2,316	2,213½*	-	156	-	156	** Includes 55½ hours overtime.
"	1926	2,039½	2,088 *	10½	-	5	15½	* Includes 4 hours overtime.
"	1927	2,211	2,125½*	2	85	½	87½	* Includes 9 hours overtime.
"	1928	2,354½	2,342½*	89½	-	½	89½	* Includes 78 hours overtime.
TOTALS........		11,223	11,022½*	101½	241	6	348½	* Includes 148½ hours overtime.

N.B.—The "Hours Works open" does not include the Works Holiday (averaging about 20 days per annum); "Special leave" represents time lost for Holidays in addition to the usual Works Holidays.

DAVID JOHN WHATLEY has completed an apprenticeship in this Department as shewn above.

He bears a good character, possesses good ability as a Mechanic, and has conducted himself in a satisfactory manner.

C.M. Collett

Chief Mechanical Engineer.

Certificate signed by C. Collett (1928) – trade: General Fitting & Machine Shop, Swindon. Another Carriage & Wagon Works example but this time from the General Fitting & Machine Shop.

EXAMPLES OF EMPLOYMENT FORMS – CARRIAGE & WAGON WORKS

The following forms trace the course of employment of an applicant for work in the Carriage & Wagon Works at Swindon. From leaving school into temporary work as a shop assistant, to application for employment as an office boy, allocated to No. 23 Workshop C&W Works Swindon, after the statutory medical

3

GREAT WESTERN RAILWAY.

TERMS OF ENGAGEMENT OF WAGES STAFF.

---

1. An employee must devote himself exclusively to the service of the Company, must reside at or near the place of his employment, attend for duty during such hours as may be required, be loyal and obedient and conform to all Rules and Regulations of the Company.

2. He must abstain from any act that may injuriously affect the interests of the Company, and, except in the proper performance of his duties must not make public or communicate to any person information concerning the business of the Company.

3. Wages will be calculated as from the day upon which duties are commenced, and will be paid weekly in the course of each following week at such times as may be convenient to the Company, subject to statutory deductions under (for example) the National Health, Pensions and Unemployment Insurance Acts, and to deductions of payments due under the Rules of any Benefit Society established or authorised by the Company. (Particulars of the existing Societies may be obtained on application).

4. Seven days' previous notice in writing of termination of service shall be given on either side, provided that in case of drunkenness, disobedience of orders, misconduct or negligence, or absence from duty without leave, the Company reserve the right to dismiss an employee without notice.

5. No wages will be payable in respect of periods of absence from duty.

6. These terms of engagement will continue to apply throughout the period of employee's service with the Company, subject to any agreed variations.

Great Western Railway: Terms of Engagement of Wages Staff.

A copy of the terms of engagement is to be handed to the accepted candidate.

4,000-12.36-(17)/—P.O.

examination, to employment in No. 9 Shop as an apprentice coach trimmer, in the later 1930s, then involved in the Second World War in the Royal Electrical Mechanical Engineers (1944–45), and resuming employment in 1945, with the allowed 'No Break of Service', as a coach trimmer.

Great Western Railway: Application for Employment on the Wages Staff.

Great Western Railway: Medical Certificate for Wages Staff.

GREAT WESTERN RAILWAY. (3841)

Reference No. *T3505*

APPLICATION FOR TEMPORARY EMPLOYMENT.

1058. (TERMINABLE BY ONE DAY'S NOTICE).

Name in full *Ivor Francis Hayward*

Address *120, Cricklade Rd., Swindon.*

Date of Birth *15/2/23 (22)* — Married or Single *Single*

Height .... Weight ....

Class of Employment desired *Coach Trimming.*

*Reason for leaving last employment *See below.*

Whether previously employed by G.W.R. *Yes. 1058 No.9 Shop. Coach Trimmer's Appr.*
If so, where, in what capacity, between *14/11/38 - 20/8/HH * D.C.O.A.*
what dates, and cause of leaving?

Has applicant at any time sustained a
rupture or other injury? If so, give *See P.V. Cards. Regd. No. H879.*
date and full particulars

Has applicant received compensation in
respect of any injury? If so, state *Ord. Comp.*
if lump sum and give amount *No*

Does applicant suffer from varicose veins? *No*

Particulars of service with Colours, if any *1/10/42 - 8/3/45. R.C.M.C. *Med. Cat.*

State if enrolled in Territorials, Army } *No.*
Air Force, or Navy Reserve }
Would applicant be prepared to accept employment } *Yes.*
on any part of the Company's system?

I hereby certify that the above statements and the particulars given on the back of the form are strictly accurate, and, if accepted for employment, I undertake to conform to all the rules and regulations of the Company, and I agree that no wages will be payable in respect of periods of absence from duty.

Applicant's signature *I F Hayward* — Date *6/3/45*

* Particulars of previous employment should be inserted on the back of the form.

For Official Use :— *Resumed duty with Co, 12/3/45. 7.58 a.m.*

If services required, state probable duration of employment ....

Date commenced work *No break in Service with the Co* Grade *Coach Trimmer.*

Department **CARR. & WAGON.** Station **SWINDON.**

Rate of pay *HH + H3/6. W.W.*

Signature *For E. T. J. EVANS* Date *1.3.45*

25,000—B.M. 36—1941—(17)—S

Great Western Railway: Application for Employment of Staff for Temporary Service and Replacement of Staff Serving with HM Forces.

TIME RECORDING AND PAYMENT METHODS – HOW DID THEY DO IT?

In the steam years, employees in the industry, as in all others, were strictly controlled regarding adherence to working hours and this was of paramount importance if employment was to be continued. Flexible working was unheard of and lateness was not tolerated.

Many industries, as well as the railways, had developed systems based on the employees taking a metal 'check' or 'tally' off a numbered board on starting a shift and returning it when the shift finished. The photographs illustrating this show the various designs of the metal checks, some in different metals to show a different use. Shapes were of several designs, each for a specific use or location. These, taking the case of Swindon Works, recorded the comings and goings of a workforce of many thousands, each workshop maintaining a register of all employed within.

The shift timing, again taking Swindon Works, was controlled by timed blasts on the factory steam 'hooter' or siren – three blasts at five-minute intervals to start the shift and one blast to finish. If the individual had not removed his check when the last starting blast faded away the cover on the board containing all the checks, on individual numbered hooks, was slammed down and the individual was deemed 'late'. A few minutes late and the unfortunate was recorded in the time book and would lose a quarter of an hour's pay. Over a quarter-hour and up to half an hour and the loss would be half an hour's pay and when more than that a shiny, aluminium disc with the words '*See Foreman before starting*' was placed on his check hook. This was to be avoided at all costs, as the foreman could send the worker home for the complete shift. Too many recurring lateness episodes and the employee would receive a small form with name, shop and check number, and the legend '*From* [date] *your services are no longer required*'.

With the check system there were a number of checks for different recorded information: ¼ or ½ for lost pay; 'OS' if the check could not be removed as the worker was away from the Works i.e. 'Out of Station'; 'N' showed the operator was 'On Night' Shift; 'CTO' showed the worker was working temporarily off the Works premises and was allowed to book in at the 'Central Time Office'; 'MT' indicated the employee had mislaid or lost his check and 'Missing Ticket' was recorded. Below is one example of working hours strictness!

PAYMENT SYSTEMS (AND ASSOCIATED PROBLEMS)

In addition to the normal 'wage' paid to the employees, the early twentieth century saw the introduction of a 'piecework' system whereby each job was allocated a small sum of money as a bonus.

Each 'chargehand' of the working groups controlled the gang and the work, and 'signed the contract' with the supervision for the gang's working week, a procedure which soon became an accepted routine. The piecework prices were recorded in a gang register, which became the gang bible, being closely guarded from the chargehand of the next gang, and the prices never discussed.

Booking the piecework amounts per week was very closely watched by both supervision and chargehand. In some instances a particularly good week when the work had gone smoothly with no particular snags was carefully balanced with those weeks when problems had occurred, and some jobs were listed from a 'good week' in the 'back of the book', to be claimed when a poor week required balancing to roughly equal the weekly average. Any overbooking could result in prices being reduced – a situation to be avoided at all costs. Thus the weekly totals were closely watched, referred to by the gang with the ubiquitous question 'What's the balance this week?'

Prices were based on a nominal time factor for doing any particular job, a time not recorded in the register, and not established by any 'stopwatch'. It would appear that he who shouted the loudest got the best values in the discussions over prices between chargehands and foremen, based on times claimed. However, there came a time in the 1950s when modernisation raised its head, and it became obvious to all that drastic changes were becoming essential. The steam locomotives and associated Carriage & Wagon rolling stock and their many piecework covered components were about to be phased out and the I/C-engined locomotives were starting to arrive. This situation triggered some far-thinking proposals by the Great Western's management and a firm of industrial consultants was contracted to examine working practices applying the two main components of the techniques of 'Work Study', namely 'Work Measurement' and 'Method Study', coupled with a Survey of Organisation of the costing system and management function, with a check on productivity with the object of overall improvement.

Two 'Work Study' managers were appointed, one Loco Works, one Carriage & Wagon Works, and three recruits were selected from the technical workforce for training in applying those techniques by the consultants, and all were started at the BR Work Study School located at Paddington – I was one of the three recruits – two from the Carriage & Wagon Works and one from the Loco Works (this was 1955).

From the training so received, it soon became obvious to those undergoing the course that an earthquake was about to shake Swindon Works (and the railways generally) as considerably less facilities would be required for the continuation of the railway power-traction construction and maintenance, and anything which 'didn't pay' was out, including the tracks and routes themselves. This was a very early move by the Great Western, in an effort to be the first in 'modernisation'. It was now essential to update and upgrade everything that could be, to retain as much as possible before those works which couldn't keep up were phased out.

And now the problems began, particularly with the Loco Works. The dominant Works committee union, the Amalgamated Engineering Union (AEU), flatly refused to discuss updating, and objected to any mention of productivity, particularly 'increased productivity' and using any of the work study techniques for which the consultants had been appointed. A number of meetings over several months had the same results: flat refusal to cooperate, and threats of strike action if forced to accept.

There was a slight easing of the problem in the Carriage & Wagon Works where a small embryo 'Production Control' scheme was introduced for a small component run, and a look at organisation in the Drawing Office, but, all in all, it was not developed any further and the Works involvement in updating had reached a dead end, with the management presumably 'soft pedalling' on the problem.

An example, which indicated continuing problems, came with the introduction of new requirements in production as the steam locomotives were phased out and diesel and hydraulic work was phased in. It was at this point that the 'who-does-what' disputes began between the various unions. In the Carriage & Wagon Works a new German Copy lathe was introduced. The profile Carriage & Wagon of axles was determined by an accurate former or pattern, which the cutting tool followed. Who should operate the lathe? A turner or a machinist? These two positions were two different employment grades. As a result of the dispute, the new machine stayed idle for upwards of two years.

Both Carriage & Wagon Works and the Locomotive Works got involved in the debate. Locomotive construction had also changed completely. Who would do certain panel work? Carriage body makers, sheet metal workers, ex-boiler makers, fitters? Who would screw in certain screws? Coach finishers, coach builders, fitters? And so on. The Works staggered on, along with the piecework system, and the he-who-shouts-loudest method continued alongside. The hired consultants gave up, and the trained team, now moved out into the Regional Area introducing incentive schemes to 'outdoor machinery' staff with planned maintenance and servicing pumping, electrical equipment, water softening plants, lifting tackle, based on work study techniques. The thin end of an obvious wedge had been inserted into the future of Swindon Works! And all thoughts of early modernisation had been rejected. Now began a virtual inevitable train of events, still lost on the unions, and presumably the management with steam gone, and with the residue of Carriage & Wagon Work transferred to the empty steam workshops, the new work and main operations of the Carriage & Wagon work was transferred to other BR workshops and the Carriage & Wagon Works eventually closed completely in 1964. The wedge had broadened, and the rest of the Works followed (1987), when the complete Works closed down, having finished with a nondescript range of odd orders (which presumably none of the other regional workshops wanted) to be completed by a reducing staff. So ended the masterpiece of Brunel and Gooch – Swindon's Railway Works.

SHOP INSPECTORS AND PIECEWORK CHECKERS

1. A Shop Inspector who does not perform any piecework checking duties is directly responsible to the Foreman.

2. A Shop Inspector who also performs piecework checking duties is generally responsible to the Foreman, but so far as his piecework checking is concerned is also responsible to the Manager's Chief Piecework Clerk.

3. A Piecework Checker solely engaged on piecework checking is generally responsible to the Manager's Chief Piecework Clerk, but is still under the supervision of the Shop Foreman.

4. Piecework prices must first be agreed between the Shop Foreman and the men concerned, and then passed through to the Manager's Piecework Office for ratification and registration.

5. As a principle no work must be booked before it is viewed. In cases where it is impossible to see the work without hindering the job, the attention of the Manager's Piecework Office must be drawn to it in order to regularise the omission.

6. No alteration must be made to the Piecework Orders unless the alteration bears the initials of a responsible person. Erasures are not allowed.

7. Pocket books are only permitted as an aid to memory, and are not accepted as official documents. Any notes must be made as soon as possible on the recognised forms.

8. No certificate for payment of work done must be issued unless it is in accordance with the description and price in the Piecework Price Book.

9. The attention of the Manager's Piecework Office should at once be called to any discrepancy in order that it may be corrected.

10. If the Chargeman and Checker are unable to agree about the proportion to be paid for uncompleted work (½,¼ or otherwise) the Checker is to ask the Foreman to judge between them and initial for the quantity he decides upon.

11. If a Chargeman neglects to obtain a certificate for work done during the fortnight in which it should have been given, special permission will be obtained from me before a certificate is issued for payment in any subsequent fortnight.

12. No certificate should be issued until the order has been countersigned by the Manager's Piecework Office.

These instructions are for those supervising the introduction of a 'piecework' pay system.

Nov. 6th. 1916

Instructions to Piecework Checkers.

1)   As a principle no work must be booked before it is viewed. In those cases where it is impossible to see without hindering the work my attention must be called to them in order to regularise the omission.

2)   No alteration must be made to that part of piecework orders written to the Foremans instructions and any necessary to the Checkers own figures must be made by crossing through, rewriting, and initialling. Erasions are not allowed.

3)   Pocket books will not be recognised as an official statement of reference, and, if necessary at all are to be used only as an assistance to memory. Any such notes taken must be entered as quickly as possible on a recognised form.

4)   No certificate for payment of work done must be issued unless it is in accord with the price and description in the piecework price book. My attention should be at once called to any such discrepancy in order that it may be adjusted.

5)   If the Chargeman and the Checker are unable to agree about the proportion to be paid for uncompleted work ($\frac{1}{2}$, $\frac{1}{4}$ or otherwise) the Checker is to ask the Foreman to judge between them and initial for the quantity he decides upon.

6)   If a Chargeman neglects to obtain a certificate for work done during the fortnight in which it should have been given, special permission will be obtained from me before a certificate is issued for payment in any subsequent fortnight.

7)   If in the opinion of the Checker any work appears to be faulty he is to direct the Foremans attention to it. If the foreman expresses his satisfaction with the work a certificate is to be given but not otherwise.

8)   The Checker when not engaged on his primary duties will hold himself ready to assist in inspecting work to the best of his ability when desired by Foreman.

9)   If a Checker has to absent himself from work from any cause he is to advise me at once and give probable duration of absence.

C.B.Collett.

per

An example of working hours strictness!

PAYDAY

Thursday was always payday and the check on the board was copper for that shift, which also served as a timekeeping record once removed. This was the 'pay cheque' as that wording quite clearly stated (see illustrations following). On pay morning, a special table was erected in each workshop at which the shop staff queued in check number order, about ten minutes before the end of the shift, awaiting the arrival of the foreman before payout could start. The cash in small individual tins was brought to the shop by a labourer accompanied per shop by two clerks from the Pay Office. A nod from the foreman and the first check was placed on the slide and pushed into a special cylindrical tin box by the pay clerk, the second pay clerk handing over the matching pay tin with the cash and the recording payslip. Five minutes and all tins were quickly handed over, clerks disappeared and the table folded for next payday.

Collection of cash from the bank was unique in that it could never happen now. On the Thursday morning of payday, a factory transport vehicle left the Main Works entrance, an iron box trailer in tow, on which sat in the open two pay clerks, reminiscent of the 'wild west' riding shotgun – although unarmed!

At the same time, same day, same route, there and back from the bank the wages of 13,000 employees in cash in the 'iron coffin', as it was known, was transported to the Cash Office to be made up into individual amounts related to the 'pay bill' details per workshop and put in the tin. The movement through the dark yards of the Works delivering the flat black tins containing the individual pay tins were, as far as is known, never in danger of theft, or attempt from the bank. It was certainly a different age (see page 109**).**

CHECKS & CHEQUES

The Keeping And Payment Of Wages At Swindon Works

Example 'checks'.   A 'pay tin' – full size.

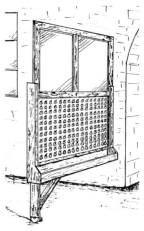

Payment for wages. The pay check was returned to the   A workshop 'check board'.
large container which had a slot in the lid.

The Swindon Works bank run, *c.* 1950: off to collect the payroll in cash from the bank – every Thursday, same time, same route – a factory transport vehicle and cash box, the 'iron coffin' trailer, are seen leaving the main entrance to the works.

A small tin, 1⅝in in diameter by 1¼in deep, containing wages used during the author's apprenticeship.

TIME RECORDING AND PAYMENT METHODS

The author's collection of various time recording checks.

A selection of 'checks' or 'cheques' used to collect wages on payday, exchanged for a 'pay tin'.

THE SWINDON WORKS EMPLOYEE

There were a number of benefits to being a GWR employee. The head of the family could obtain regular tickets for cheap coal, delivered in 1-hundredweight loads by Great Western Road Transport to the house. For 9*d*, wood offcuts and scrap from Carriage & Wagon repairs could also be obtained by cheap ticket. An allocation of free and cheap rail-travel tickets were also obtainable for the whole family. The free issue included a 'foreign free pass', and I remember being on demob leave from the RAF (tickets were still obtainable during military service, incidentally) and travelling by rail with a railway colleague to Italy at no cost. The cheap tickets obtainable were one third of the 'standard rate fare', called a 'privilege' ticket. A first-class free pass or privilege (colloquially known as 'priv') ticket was available to senior supervisory and management staff, from which I benefited during my railway service.

By far the most valuable benefit for those at Swindon Works, was the receipt of full medical care, for a small sum deducted from wage or salary. I, having benefited from my father's membership during school years for the usual mumps, measles and chickenpox ailments, acquired the same medical benefits in my own right when I joined the Works as an office boy in 1944, for the princely deduction from wages of 4*d* per week. Incidentally office boys' wages were 16*s* 8*d* for a fifty-hour week including Saturday mornings!

The Great Western facilities included a small, fully equipped four-bed hospital, with its own operating theatre located just outside the Works itself from 1871. An A&E Department and several GPs in a separate building known as the 'Medical Fund' with an extensive dispensary for various pills and medication, at no extra cost, with usually short queues at the dispensing windows. The service also included home visits by the GPs. The building also housed two swimming baths, a Turkish bath section as well as a full dental treatment section. It was this complete service on which our National Health Service was based!

THE LAST DECADES TO CLOSURE

The new production and repair programmes were listed during the 1940s steam years as approximately 300 passenger vehicles per year constructed and 5,000 repairs of varying levels, with around 5,000 new wagons built per year and around 16,000 repaired. Classes of repairs of all vehicles included about one third of all coaches and over a half of all wagons requiring a heavy or major repair, continuing after nationalisation.

The manning level of the Carriage & Wagon Works was about 5,000. Construction of both carriages and wagons had developed over the years to include coaching stock up to 70ft long, with a massive array of wagon designs far bigger than those of the early years, with riveting of metal components being overtaken by developments of both carriages and wagons into the realms of welded construction; both gas and arc now in use for the new work as opposed to only repairs, with steel replacing the traditional wood usage for panelling. Internally, wood was retained. The interim stage of metal panelling attached to wood framing was still in vogue in the 1940s being secured by hundreds and thousands of screws, soon to be replaced by all welded steel sheets to steel framing.

Within twenty years the Carriage & Wagon Works had closed whilst still under the shroud of nationalisation and a new era of electric and diesel locomotives and rolling stock had altered, beyond recognition, the function of Swindon Works. A few carriage and wagon jobs were relocated to empty locomotive workshops, the majority of work sent to other British Rail works.

5

THE WORKSHOPS: WHERE AND HOW THE WORK WAS DONE

The function of workshops, identifying numbers as follows during the Great Western years and nationalisation:

CARRIAGE & WAGON WORKS – Numbers identify the Shops

The C&W offices fronting No. 15 Shop, wiewed from the station.

NOS 1 & 2 SAWMILLS: AN OUTLINE HISTORY

By 1870, south of the main line, the first carriage shops were established, with the wagon shops continuing at their original 1846 site. As the Works was on a higher level than the surrounding streets, the carriage shops were thus also on a higher level and the section of the new shop allocated for a saw mill section thus had a suspended floor, with reasonable headroom under it. This space was utilised as a timber-drying and stacking area, as well as an easy way for the disposal of sawdust and shavings from the woodworking machinery above.

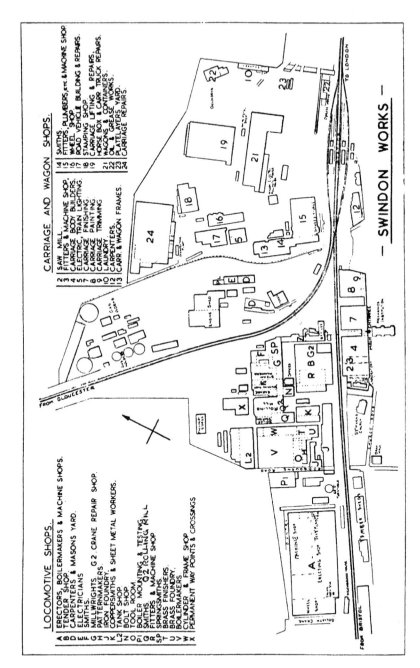

Swindon Railway Works in the Great Western steam years.

On street level, adjacent to the 'underground' area was the Fire Station Yard, where the Works' fire engines were kept with accommodation for maintenance and crews. Also in later years, towering over one corner, was the coned body of the 'cyclone', the giant vacuum cleaner which sucked up the shavings and sawdust, piped under the machinery in the mill, which had a moveable spout which also allowed it to take up and/or deliver the contents to and from rail wagons on the adjacent rail line. There was also, remembered from seventy years ago, a stationary boiler which also burned off-cuts and residue. Occupying a corner opposite the cyclone was a large boiler house with a furnace which also burned residue from the mill.

This area brings back another memory, which could have signalled the end of my railway career before it had begun. As the office boy for the Timber Stores office, I often visited the little area into which off-cuts of wood were sent down a short chute to be handled by two old employees who weighed them in one hundredweight bundles, which could be purchased by employees for 9*d* exchanged for a pre-purchased ticket. From the Sawmill above, a narrow sloped path led down into the yard. It was part of my job to take paperwork down to the Sales Office and on one occasion I ran up the slope carrying my paper satchel over my shoulder, and straight across the lines between two wagons at the top of the slope. I was just stepping over the further rail when, completely unknown to me and not indicated in any way, the shunting of the wagons was under way. As I stepped one foot over the second rail the wagons crashed together with an almighty bang, trapping my satchel, which I had pushed behind me as I ran, between the buffers. A step short and it could have been me! A step on and I almost collided with the mill foreman who was supervising the shunt. I have never actually seen a man go so grey in the face, as the reality settled in. The next time I saw them shunting, I found there were so many flags and warning notices on view it was like a review of the fleet!

Once the built-up area to the west had consolidated, around 1900, some of the area was already in use and No. 1 Sawmill had been established. By 1920 a Saw Maintenance Shop and a timber-drying kiln had been added. Some of the large wood-preparation mechanical saws had been removed from the 1870 workshops to deal in No. 1 Mill with the initial preparation of the tree trunks and other heavy work, with craneage to suit.

The early plank saw was really a step up from the manual saw pit, where stout fellows, one in the pit and one on the tree trunk, handled a vertical saw, not a job for the faint-hearted: physically lifting and pushing and pulling the saw for each cut – no wonder they had a reputation as heavy drinkers! The early mechanical version powered by a steam engine had closer, vertically mounted saw blades with the vertical movement of the pit saw. Developing metallurgy had allowed the very flexible band saw to replace the vertical reciprocating earlier design. This fast running flexible blade – now running for a horizontal cut, the endless loop of the blade supported by and running over two large wheels – eliminated even more of the hard work of sawing. Blades were maintained in an adjacent small workshop where various machines and the 'saw doctors' kept them sharp and the teeth set to give the required 'kerf' or width of saw cut.

Another memory from office-boy days, which really shows the dangers of any workshop practice, was that of the saws. As well as the band saw, there was also the rotating circular saw. We mentioned above the kerf and this whilst normally giving fixed width of cut, could by means of 'wobble washers' cut a wider groove. The method applied to the circular saw made it wobble so that the periphery cut a path much wider than the kerf. On my route through to the Shop Office, I stopped to watch a machinist grooving, I believe, a door pillar. As he pushed it over the saw the blade picked up the grain in the wood and threw off an 18-in 'spear' which went right through the palm of his hand. He jumped back and shook the hand, whereby the spear broke off, leaving about 6ins right through the palm. He calmly walked over to the man on the next saw and said 'Could you pull this out?' who quickly refused, and a call to the first aider immediately took him to the first aid box. After an accompanied visit to hospital for removal, a few days later, and he was back on the same job. All certainly interesting for a 14-year-old office boy! There were also a number of men with part or all of a finger missing! I believe the use of 'wobble washers' is now prohibited … but the requirement of wood sawing, of course, continues.

TIMBER CUTTING AND SEASONING: WHY WOOD TWISTS AND WARPS

Most quality woods currently are used for veneers and the traditional method of 'quarter sawing' (see sketch below) is now often only used for the highest quality timbers, as it is both more wasteful than other methods and more time consuming. Wood sections produced by more economical methods such as 'through and through' or 'billet' sawn (see 1–5 below) are less wasteful in the initial stages of cutting, but problems of warping and shakes can occur on seasoning. As such, the use of this type of wood entails further careful selection, cutting and finishing and thus time and costs escalate.

The modern method of quarter sawing is shown in sketch 2, which has a certain economic advantage, and also boxes out the 'heart' of the log with its softer core. This method also produces some planks cut as traditional quarter-sawn (the soft core wood is not normally used).

Plain sawn also boxes out a bad heart section, but introduces some of the problems of 'through-and-through' cutting with the potential of very bad distortion of the top and bottom cuts (sketch 4).

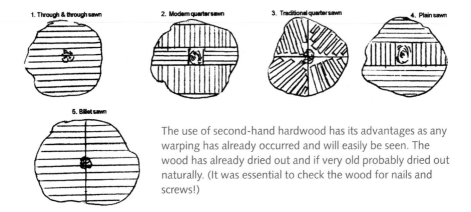

The use of second-hand hardwood has its advantages as any warping has already occurred and will easily be seen. The wood has already dried out and if very old probably dried out naturally. (It was essential to check the wood for nails and screws!)

SEASONING

Removal or dry out of the natural sap in the timber is done by one of two ways:

Natural seasoning – entails setting the sawn boards, with spacers between each board to allow free circulation of air, within a roofed but open area, with minimum walls under the roof, again to allow free circulation.

Kiln drying – when fully controlled, ensures uniform drying of the timber but can lead to problems if incorrectly done. Usually steam heated sealed cylinders have wood packed in, but again allowing for circulation of air. Over-kilning makes the wood very light in weight and seemingly 'dead' to the touch. Over-kilned wood will absorb moisture when used and can quickly start to rot.

During the steam years, the Timber Storage Yards were kept fully stocked and drying out was a natural and lengthy process. The following is a quote from an account published in *c.* 1890 by a visitor to Swindon Works. (From *Round the Works of our Great Railways*, Various authors):

Perhaps the woodworking department is the most captivating part of the whole Works. Great trunks of oak and teak are operated on in wholesale fashion; large saws, fastened side-by-side so as to act simultaneously, converting a baulk quickly into so many plants of required thickness. Here is one man (operating a special lathe) turning elliptical pick handles; another operating a band saw cutting out ovals and rounded parallelograms for the moulded decoration of the carriage interiors; while a third attends the machine which does the moulding in the pieces of board previously prepared.

And what a wonderful machine that is! Imagine an iron table with nothing on it but one solitary steel spindle, standing up like a nine pin. The piece to be moulded is laid flat on the table, its edge pressed and pushed along against the nine pin, and behold, from the shavings and sawdust flying around in a whirlwind, it transpires that the innocent-looking spindle is really a most formidable tool, revolving at incredible speed, its cutter being the exact counterpart of the mould to be produced. Where it works with or against the grain makes no difference to this machine, the resulting mould proving to be equally smooth and uniform.

A very flowery description of a spindle moulder! The visitor continues in the same vein:

That this moulded work is of mahogany is not surprising, considering that it is intended for ornamentation; but what is rather surprising is that some of the other wood work, which is not moulded, and which in its finished state will be covered with paint, is made of mahogany also. So lavish seems to be the use of this material, that even the outside panels of the carriages below the windows are made of it; inferior wood appears to be nothing accounted of even as in the days of Solomon.

So, it would appear that nothing but the best was in use for the Great Western's carriage stock, a reflection of the thinking of the time in an age of plenty, but which has left a difficult legacy for modernity to follow.

NO. 1 SAWMILL

Most of the timber was received in log form, to be cut into usable format and to be further cut into the many wood sections required for carriages and wagons and for other general carpentry, including pattern making.

The 'usable' format has to be first seasoned before further use, and to speed the drying process a timber drying kiln was installed during the 1930s comprising a Sturtevant Seasoning Plant which used the three essential operations: air circulation, heat and moisture control. It takes many months to season wood naturally, but the new plant speeded up the process considerably. This artificial seasoning of timber takes the form of four separate compartments. Placed on trolleys with 'spacers' between the wood pieces, it is pulled by hand winch into the kiln. Each compartment is separately controlled externally by steam jets and fans to ensure correct heat and humidity was maintained and the amount of timber which can be dried at a setting is 8,000ft. Conversion of the logs and trees into usable pieces is done by a pair of log band saws, one horizontal and one vertical; the vertical was of American source. Lifting the timber baulks was done by an overhead 10-ton crane.

All saw blades are maintained by a 'saw doctor' section, who also undertakes sharpening of planes, thicknessing and tenoning cutters.

It was recorded in 1949 that 2,776 logs were handled and converted for work of all classes throughout Swindon Carriage & Wagon and Loco Works.

A selection of heavy-duty reciprocating and band saws c. 1950.

The first phase of the preparation of timber c. 1890.

No. 1 Sawmill.

Timber Yard, No. 1 Sawmill.

No. 1 Sawmill.

NO. 2 SAWMILL

This was the original site for timber preparation; the increased quantities had necessitated the building of No. 1 Sawmill, and No. 2 was now the finishing mill, utilising the seasoned wood for the many components now required by the Works and with a full range of woodworking machine tools.

The timber followed a set course through the shop, first prepared into the basic sizes for the many uses to which now follow. This included such operations as band sawing, planing, thicknessing, shaping, boring, mortising, rounding (wood lathes and specially adapted turning for various handles, hammer, pick etc. of oval form), tenoning, rebating and wood bending. This latter was a fascinating procedure to watch, which I did as an office boy in 1944! There were two Fay & Eagan (American) wood-bending machines, associated with separate steaming cylinders.

Wood to be bent, usually roof hoops for carriage roof construction, were first steam soaked in the cylinders for several hours, removed after a set period and placed on the bed of the bending machine on top of a flexible steel plate. Above the table secured to the machine was a wood former made to the shape of the required bent wood.

In operation, both bed halves of the machine table moved upward from the outer ends, forcing the wood round the former when the flexible metal plate was locked by a bar across the flat top of the former. Firmly secured in the bent position and several square section lengths of steamed wood had been bent together, the whole arrangement was slid off the former and placed aside to cool and set. It was only rarely that one length split during the process.

The railway lines of the steam years were held into the 'chairs' by a wood-shaped key. Once again it was fascinating watching the machine which fashioned the individual tapered keys produced to shape, and stamped automatically with the particular type identity number, churned out continuously from lengths of oak fed into one end of the machine. The keys coming out at the other end formed a continuous stream, one pushing the next onto a ramp up into an open goods wagon. Literally millions must have been made in this way, to be replaced by a different system using different flat bottom rails, different chairs and spring steel keys or clips. Progress!

There was also a saw-doctor facility for sharpening all saw blades and the many machine cutters.

No. 2 Sawmill: A wood-bending machine for steam-softened wood.

An early view of No. 2 Sawmill. Note: underfloor machine drives and shavings disposal.

No. 2 Sawmill: A double-tenon cutting machine.

No. 2 Sawmill.

No. 2 Sawmill.

NO. 3 FITTING & MACHINING SHOP

This was a small enclave located between No. 2 Sawmill and No. 4 Coach Body Shop in the area to the south of the main line. By the 1940s, a great deal of steel had been introduced to carriage construction, and No. 3 Shop dealt with the metal items and forms which required finishing touches before fitting to the No. 4 Shop Coaches.

By 1950 one of the main jobs was the preparation of the sixteen-gauge metal sheets (now galvanised) to cover the sides, roofs and ends of the coaches. There was the necessary selection of machine tools, including guillotines, multiple punches (when the coaches had wooden framing, the sheets were pre-punched for the thousands of screw holes as well as automatically countersunk to ensure the screw head was below the level of the plate face), but welding construction was now coming to the fore.

Among the machine tools was the 90-ton British Clearing Press, which did much of the multi-punching of the larger metal sections such as the coach body sides. The machines were maintained by the shops' fitters, as was the machine complement in the complete Carriage & Wagon Workshops on the south side of the main line, including the machinery in No. 1 Sawmill. The section also dealt with the repairs to the smaller metal fittings used in coach bodies, brackets, door hinges and fittings such as door handles and locks.

No. 3 Coach Component Fitting & Machining Shop.

NO. 4 CARRIAGE BODY BUILDING SHOP

By the 1940s the underframe and much of the body were built in steel, thus the outside of the coach was virtually fireproof. Wood was retained for the internal structures as in the main body framework to which the external steel panels were screwed. As an office boy (1944–46) in the Timber Stores office which was in a corner of the No. 4 Shop, I have a lasting memory of the smell of tallow which pervaded the shop as every screw inserted in the panels was dipped in the tin of tallow found on every bench. Welding must have taken much of the fun from the building of coach bodies as tallow seemed to find its way onto all the hand tools used.

The wood sections came through from No. 2 Sawmill and from No. 3 Shop came all of the increasing metal work required, including the steel panels for the sides, ends and roof of coaching stock. The carriage bodies were assembled to the 'rolling chassis' of the underframe, run-in between platforms set at buffer level, and once positioned the doors could be fitted when the body had settled.

In the early days of my employment, I was invited on several occasions to put in a screw or two. Enthusiasm soon faded when complaints at home referred to the smell of tallow! But it wouldn't have done to have missed it.

NO. 4 COACH BODY SHOP

Whilst passengers had, from the early years, taken their own sandwiches and food hampers aboard to refresh themselves during the journey, the Great Western, in 1896, introduced the first two restaurant cars for first-class passengers. This facility had developed by 1900 into designs for central gangways and a kitchen car for refreshments brought to tables between seats – by 1903 there were restaurant cars for all three classes of travel. This stopped, however, in 1917 due to war exigencies, but was again reinstated in 1919. The story of the first restaurant cars follows with a contemporary page from the *Great Western Magazine*, which also shows details of carriage construction *c.*1900 as well as the car story – the construction view is exactly as I remembered it as an office boy in 1944. Note in the car construction the doorway is in the end of the carriage for gangway construction and access to the next carriage by means of the now familiar 'concertina' for flexible access from coach to coach.

Coach construction.

142   GREAT WESTERN RAILWAY MAGAZINE.

Carriage Department.

Of the thousands of people who day by day travel in ease and comfort in the Company's luxurious coaching stock, probably few give more than a passing thought to the elaboration involved, first in designing the vehicles and secondly in building them up stage by stage into the elegant finished article. I, therefore, venture to think that the series of unique photographs (taken specially for the MAGAZINE by Mr. Churchward's kind permission), here reproduced, will prove interesting and give a good idea of the method of building a carriage. The views show one of the Company's new restaurant cars in three initial stages of construction in the body shop at Swindon.

No. 1 depicts the floor framing with the pillars driven in to ascertain if the mortises are correct.

No. 2 shows the pillars in their permanent positions and the side framing built, without roof.

No. 3 shows the hoop sticks in position over the roof, and the panelling and moulding on the sides and ends.

After the roof has been fixed, the body is practically complete. It is then, as a rule, wheeled, and transferred to the paint shop, where it is subjected to the operations of the finishers and trimmers, who equip the carcase with its various members, the complete vehicle passing finally into the hands of the painters. The skeleton views are supplemented (*see* frontispiece) by interior and exterior views of the vehicle in its finished state.

These restaurant cars, of which two will shortly be put into service, constitute a departure from standard practice in one important item, as will

be gathered from the following description. Their length over body is 70 feet, and width 9 feet; the height from floor to roof, which is of the elliptical pattern, being 8 feet. The body is carried on a steel underframe, supported on four-wheeled bogies of the bolster type, with elliptic springs on the bolsters. The bogies have a wheel base of 9 feet, and are fitted with balance beams over the boxes which carry the double coil springs. Seating accommodation is provided for forty-two passengers of all classes. The kitchen and pantry are at one end of the cars, and are provided with stoves, plate racks, cupboards, wine cellars, etc. In the vestibule nearest the kitchen, also in the corridor, are cupboards, refrigerator, etc., for the proper storage of food. The passenger compartment is divided by a partition containing transparent photographs, a novel and extremely pleasing introduction, the opening in the partition being screened by a curtain. Seating is arranged for two on one side and one on the other, leaving a corridor 2 feet 7 inches wide. These compartments have net rods each side and are provided with chairs of the ordinary moveable type, upholstered in Spanish Antique

BUILDING A RAILWAY CARRIAGE.

Buffalo leather, this form of seating constituting the departure from standard practice already mentioned. The compartments are fitted with polished walnut framing and veneer panels, the roof being cased with lincrusta, lined out in gold. Fourteen tables, also of polished walnut, inlaid with green Morocco leather, are provided, seven being double and the same number single.

GWR Magazine: this contemporary page illustrates building methods.

The STEAM museum exhibit showing wooden coach construction methods and design.

Roof hoop sticks were steamed and shaped from one piece of wood on a special machine in an annex to the sawmill.

Construction showing the reinforcing metal corner brackets.

Corner of No.4
(Body) Shop.

No. 4 Coach Body Shop, 1944. As a 14-year-old office boy, I remember the Timber Stores office in a corner of Swindon's No. 4 Body Shop, with its wood framed, iron sheeted carriages under repair and the foul smell of tallow, into which every screw was dipped before insertion (c. 1944). A tallow tin on every bench.

In three years, nationalisation was to pull a shroud over the face of the Great Western, although for a short time everything carried on as before. Note: through the open door the area covered by a traversing table to move the coaches across into the Paint Shop. The steps down have a folding guardrail arrangement and lead down to the main 'tunnel entrance' to the Works.

No. 4 Coach Body Shop.

No. 4 Coach Body
Shop.

No. 4 Body Shop:
welding construction.

No. 4 Body Shop.

NO. 5 SHOP – ELECTRICAL MAINTENANCE

This shop dealt with all of the electrical equipment associated with coaches and other rolling stock. It comprised a three-section workshop, dealing with (a) fitting, turning and test bed section, (b) a battery repair area and (c) a battery charging facility.

By 1950 there were approaching 6,000 electrically equipped carriages all to be maintained, within a shop capable of maintaining all electricity-generating equipment with regulating and other control gear for an output of 260 coaches per year. Reconditioned carriage-lighting dynamos were run on test for two hours. A carriage lighting battery was of considerable size, weighing in at 1,800lbs, and contained twelve (approximately) 10in x 7in x 17in deep Pilkington glass cells each containing nine positive plates, with a capacity of 240 amp hours at 24 volts. 80,000 of such glass cells were in use at this period. Also at this time, special equipment in a number of coaches produced Hi-cycle AC current for fluorescent lighting, with equipment for refrigeration and radio.

No. 5 Shop.

No. 5 Electrical Shop: carriage lighting dynamos on test.

No. 6 Shop (Paint).

No. 7 Finishing Shop: the 'Two-man Sub'.

NO. 6 SHOP

This had been the Carriage Repair Shop which had been superseded to a great extent by the opening in 1927 of the new No.24 shop complex and by 1950 the main six-shop operation had been replaced by the installation of special mixing machines which prepared 'Swindon Fireproof Flooring Composition', a cement-like material for use in the floor installation in new luggage vans and the older coaching stock repairs.

NOS 7A, 7B, 7C, 24B & 24C SHOPS

These closely associated shops dealt with most of the major internal coach items. The No. 24 Shop pair, b and c, handled quarter light and door windows, seat back frames, all doors, lavatory, corridor and gangway doors, panelling, luggage racks and all woodwork associated with electric lighting, with the final touches added in 24c, the Polishing Shop. These components are then sent for installation in No. 4 Body Shop.

No. 7 Finishing Shop.

No. 7 Finishing Shop.

Greatly assisting in this production run, reducing times of item construction, was an 800-ton Shaw Veneer Press. This machine could be used 'hot or cold' having steam-heated hot plates. Pressures used were about 150lbs per square inch, and the hot plates were 7ft 6in x 6ft 6in. Hydraulic supply pressure was from the 800lbs per square inch works main. (This was the lower of the two mains, the other being 1500lbs per square inch.) The work varied from all classes of doors, shaped and flat, to that of large roof covings. Work was passed on to others in the group for polishing etc., and doors were returned to the shop for fittings, locks etc. to be attached.

NO. 7C SHOP

This shop dealt with all items requiring a high-gloss finish. The use of cellulose lacquers, applied by brush to the wood components, also used were the standard French polish, along with other colour items to match the growing use of plastics in the interior finishing of coaches.

NO. 10A SHOP

This was an all-female shop undertaking such jobs as glass, chromium plate and felt cleaning, and in addition to the French polishing of small items they also sorted recycled screws, which were cleaned, relacquered and packed for return to stores and reuse. This latter was a surprising salvage job which, to be recorded at all, must have given substantial savings.

NOS 8, 21B & 24 SHOPS

The late 1940s saw a major change in the colour schemes. This was the transition period, the end of the Great Western and the introduction of the Western Region colour schemes. In 1949, out of 1,341 coaches painted in Nos 8 and 24 Shops, 120 new coaches were painted in the crimson and cream colours of the nationalisation era.

Whilst interior panel spraying with cellulose was introduced, there was a considerable amount of smaller items which were stove enamelled. Painted and lettered, the yearly output of coach destination boards averaged 1,500.

The now well-established Paint Mill, although old, still had a good production output for painting all rolling stock including locomotives. Manufacture of the various paints was from either paste or dry colours, and a late 1948 output is recorded as: 'from paste in oil: 761 tons and ground in oil from dry colours: 111 tons'. A surprising amount of putty was produced, 27 tons.

In 21b Shop, painters of wagons applied canvas to roofs, canvas pre-treated with special oil, an annual output of the oil mix amounting to 12,735 gallons. There were various mixes of cleaning oils for exterior and interior use being an average annual use of over 65,000 and 4,500 gallons respectively.

Repaired motor and horse drawn vehicles repaired in No. 17 Shop were also painted in the shop by staff from No. 24 Shop.

NOS 9, 9A & 19A SHOPS – THE TRIMMING DEPARTMENT

No. 9 Shop – this dealt with all materials ranging from upholstery leather work e.g. window straps, axle box lubricating pads, straps for artificial limbs (the limbs also made in-house), water column bags, repairs to hose pipes, and was an all-male shop.

No. 9a Shop – was an all-female shop operating sewing machines, repairing and making blinds, curtains, bedding for the railway hotels and furniture upholstery. Incidentally, approximately 340 tons of recovered upholstery horsehair was dealt with annually, carded and cleaned for reuse.

No. 19a Shop – this shop dealt with carriage upholstery and trimmings, roofs of coaches, gangways and side screens for road vehicles. The use of the special disinfecting unit was a major step forward, the plant itself is illustrated on page 172 killing off any vermin or germs.

NO. 10 SHOP – LAUNDRY

This was also a female-operated shop handling over 1,900,000 items per year, utilising six washing machines, four electric hydros, a tumble dryer and two six-roll calendars. Dry-cleaning facilities were also available and there were sixteen drying ovens.

NO. 11 SHOP – GENERAL LABOURERS

This group was responsible for all shunting operations in the yards south of the mainline and movements of all new and repaired coaches through the relevant shops. When completed, the coach moved by the shunting engine for all vacuum testing, battery attention, changing if required, and a general clean before being released for entry into traffic. Movements to and from the Lifting Shop, all movements of coal and coke and all shunting in connection with timber movement and a material handling from outstation for repairs both receipt and despatch, were covered, with all clearance of wagons from the Loco Yard.

Early view of Trimming Shop No. 9.

No. 9 Trimming Shop: upholstery making.

No. 9 Trimming Shop.

No. 9 Trimming Shop: the sewing group.

No. 9 Trimming Shop.

No. 9 Trimming Shop: making artificial limb straps etc. for injured GW employees.

No. 12 Carpenters' Shop.

No. 12 Carpenters' Shop: furniture making and repair.

NO. 12 SHOP – CARPENTERS

This shop had quite a variety of different duties, which included making and repairing all furniture for railway office use and station waiting rooms as well as, at the other end of the scale, sack trucks, coach battery boxes and platform trolleys. The battery boxes were well made; the dovetail joints, cut with the precision of a Robinson Box Dovetailing Machine's multiple high-speed cutters, were used for all box joints and drawers. Other machines include routers for jig shaping, mortising and boring amongst other jobs. There was a small No. 12a Shop for polishing items to finish.

NO. 13A SHOP

This shop had benefited from the reduction in the riveting process to include welding in construction of carriage frames. Steel components were passed through various processes for straightening, milling and drilling, with sole bars and longitudinals passed again through the straightening procedure to introduce a set $^7/_8$in camber before passing on for assembly. With the introduction of steel, welding had and was replacing a certain amount of woodwork, and the frames were squared up using a 'piano wire' technique to set the pillars before welding. The introduction of welding also speeded the use of steel for the cant rails, which were made up in a jig in two parts and securely welded together. Multi-drilling machines greatly speeded construction before the underframe was passed on to No. 4 Body Shop.

NO. 13 SHOP

Wagon frames pass through a similar procedure to the carriage frame – all squared up and hydraulically riveted. Lifted onto the chassis for the wheels, axle boxes, tie rods, brake work and buffer, the underframe was then given a coat of red paint before being passed on to No. 21 Shop. Staffed by around 1,000 craftsmen, these shops were responsible for all designs of wagon manufacture and repair, along with road/rail transport containers, the whole being extended in production by Nos 21 and 21b Shops with welding also coming into the construction process.

No. 13 Wagon Building Shop.

No. 13 Frame Shop: Metal wagon building.

No. 13 Frame Shop: Welding wagon components.

Wood wagon repairs.

No. 13 Shop: Riveting wagon frames.

NO. 14 – SMITH'S SHOP

This is a good example of a modernisation approach to production (although probably not applauded in some circles!) The introduction of more modern machine tools and less staff allowed production to easily cover requirements. In the 1930s the only machine tools available were nine steam hammers and two 'hot' saws, soon to be updated. Originally a usual blacksmith's workshop, by the late 1940s the typical arrangement of smiths' hearths, two lines of forty along the length of the shop, had now lost one row and had been replaced by the universal welding facilities which had modernised production across the world. The welding processes now included oxy–acetylene and electric arc with the addition of a 'flash-butt welding' machine which used the two components to be welded as the usual electrode (which supplied the metal for the joint) with the 'earth', the other half of the weld joint.

No. 14 Shop: flash-butt welder.

No. 14 Smiths' Shop.

No. 14 Smiths' Shop.

By 1950 staffing was 109 as opposed to about 200 in the 1930s. There were thirty blacksmiths' forges, thirty-six oxy-acetylene welding points, six points for electric arc welding and four flash-butt welding machines.

Coupling links were made fully automatically, with preheating, flashing and final forging operations, out of control of the skill of the operator. Output, originally for coupling links using the forging skills of one blacksmith, was 180 per week. With the new machine 400 could now be produced.

Production, of course, as mentioned earlier in this book, still was controlled by the specifications issued by the Railway Clearing House for flash-butt welded chain-link couplings, and for all other requirements, such as buffers, with the drop-stamped head and shank attached by the butt welder – draw bar hooks are yet another example.

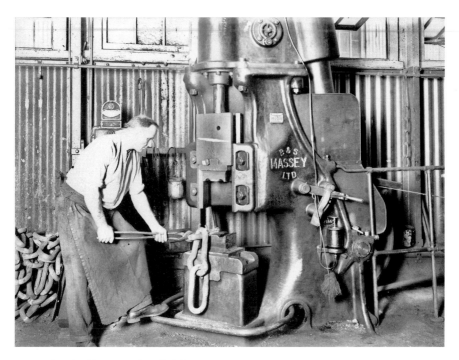

No. 14 Smiths' Shop: coupling-link forging.

No. 15 Fitting and Machining Shop.

NO. 15 – FITTING & MACHINING SHOP

The shop employed approximately 650 craftsmen in the usual trades of fitting, turning and machining and components made included vacuum brakes, axle boxes, draw gear, brake gear for wagons, steam-heating items and other miscellaneous metal fittings for both carriages and wagons. Much was produced by the standardisation process, using associated jigs and fixtures to speed up production.

A portion of the shop was set up for the manufacture of carriage frames (and bogies) up to 70ft in length; production also included special wagon frames, for example timber wagons, of similar lengths from about 45ft length upward. Traditional construction by riveting was from the war years, with the associated travelling gantry suspended hydraulic riveters, being superseded by the application of welding techniques and with extensive use of pneumatic appliances. Other items included brass and iron fittings, steam heating apparatus, corridor gangway metal fittings, and the components for carriage and wagon bogies. The Stamping Shop (No. 18) supplied the pressings and stampings, which go to the fitting benches for required drilling, milling, slotting etc. ready for assembly, then on for wheeling and springing.

NO. 15A SHOP – PLUMBERS & GAS FITTERS

Coaches, on leaving No. 4 Body Makers' Shop, still required plumbing installations and steam heating fittings. This latter included thermo-controlled radiators, connecting them to the through-steam main and passenger controls. The toilet

No. 15 Shop: final check on bogies before transfer for wheeling.

piping and facilities are also included, as is a steam-heated water supply arrangement for the washbasin. In some saloons, hot and cold showers were installed.

A combination of gas work and plumbing requirements occur in fitting out the restaurant cars, to include three-oven cooking ranges and associated hot water facilities. The complete kitchen was lined in stainless steel.

No. 15 Shop: milling cast-iron bogie centre castings.

No. 15 Shop: automatic lathes for brass bar work.

Carriage wheeling on jacks to remove or replace bogies.

No. 16 Wheel Shop during the period of the Mansell wheel.

No. 16 Wheel Shop: grinding axle journals.

NO. 16 SHOP – WHEEL ASSEMBLY

This shop deals with all wheel maintenance for carriages and wagons. Machining operations included boring, facing and turning the wheel centres with some new facilities for grinding the periphery of the running surface of the wheels. 'Work hardening' was done by hammering the rails and the rail joints, as well as by the heating and cooling of the steel surface caused by the friction of applied cast-iron brake blocks. The grinding process was also applied (the machines were double ended) to the journals once the wheel centres had been pressed on, both bearing surfaces thus ground at one setting. There were also heavy-duty lathes for turning the treads of wagon wheels, the whole process on a wheel set recorded as completed in twelve minutes.

The shop had been reorganised on a 'flow line' principle. Axle forgings entered the end of the flow, were straightened and centred and matched up to the wheel sets, which were bored. Tyres are shrunk on and secured by the Gibson ring. From the twelve minutes of wheel turning, journal grinding completed the process recorded as an average total of twenty-three minutes. The final move was to the balancing machines, where the wheels were observed and the set finalised with minimal fluctuation of the needles on the balancing dials.

Incidentally, it took a pressure of 60 tons minimum to 80 tons maximum pressure for pressing wheels onto axles, and tyres were shrunk on to the wheels with shrinkage allowances of 0.047in for carriage tyres, 0.078in for wagon tyres and 0.031in for diesel car tyres.

NO. 16A SHOP – CASE HARDENING & NORMALISING

As stated in this section's opening remarks 'normalising' returned work-hardened metal components to their original structure. This process applied to buffers, three-link couplings, drawbar links and pins, carriage and wagon items (rocking bars, hooks and couplings).

'Tempering' and 'oil quenching' entailed heating and quenching in oil or water to return certain items such as suspension bolts, instarter couplings, spring links, coupling screws, nuts and shackles, flat slings and gedge hooks to their required conditions.

'Case hardening' entailed heating to a bright red the many bolts, pins, brackets etc. which required a wear-resisting surface or case much harder than its core material, then coating it with a carbon-rich powder and quenching in water, once the surface had absorbed the covering of powder.

'Annealing' is again a heat treatment, similar to 'normalising'.

Turning the running periphery of re-tyred wheel sets.

NO. 17 SHOP – ROAD WAGON REPAIRS

For many years the Great Western's road traffic was powered by the horse and so there were extensive facilities for the care of the animals, including a big brick building at Didcot where all the animal feedstuffs were mixed (the building known as the Provender Store – now demolished) covering all the Great Western's requirements. The road wagons were a familiar sight in railway environs, delivering goods all over adjacent areas, made and maintained by the Great Western along with handcarts, two-wheel hand trucks and the well known platform four-wheel trolleys. From the 1940s and into the 1950s, horse transport was progressively replaced by motor transport – the three-wheel 'Scarab' vans a familiar sight delivering in railway areas. The road motor transport also maintained in-house for routine servicing with major road vehicle work based at Slough.

The work had expanded from the repair of the usual horse-drawn vehicles with an increasing number of motor van requirements. There was a growing requirement for specialist van bodies to suit the pre-purchased chassis for motor road vehicles – at this period 3-ton Morris or Thorneycroft designs. The bodies used 'ply max' panels with metal wood-filled roof hoops. A pool of these bodies was retained at Swindon for renewals. The shop had all of the usual woodworking carpentry facilities.

No. 17 Shop: horse wagon repair (road vehicles).

No. 17 Shop: Early Road Wagon Shop – building and repairs.

No. 17 Shop: the road transport maintained by the Great Western – not forgetting the horse!

No. 17 Shop: other transport was part of the responsibility here.

No. 17 Shop: continuing the maintenance responsibilities.

No. 17 Shop: the Scammel 'Scarab' road transport.

No. 18 Stamping Shop.

No. 18 Stamping Shop.

NO. 18 STAMPING SHOP

The main output was stampings and drop forgings for wagon frames, but also included all brake work, carriage underframes, bogies, vacuum cylinders, signal items for the Reading Signal Works, some stampings for the Locomotive Works, hot brass pressings for boiler and bogie work, forgings for jig, tool and machine repairs, and all manner of pressings for wagon bodies, including the framing, stanchions and brackets.

The building was 300ft x 300ft, with an associated Die Shop and a hydraulic Pump House which supplied the whole of the Carriage Works north of the mainline. In the building, the 300ft x 210ft Stamp Shop contained an impressive

No. 18 Stamping Shop: a
range of steam and pneumatic
hammers.

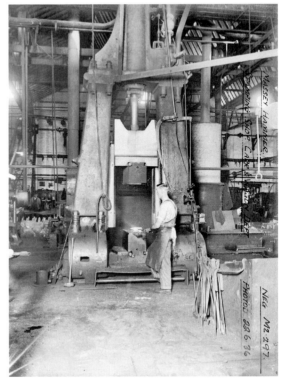

array of machine tools: nine Massey steam drop stamps, five electric drop hammers, and for forging work, there were twenty-two 5 x 10cwt hydraulic presses, which ranged between 25 and 200 tons, plus punches and shears. There were also a variety of furnace types: eleven coal-fired, five gas-fired, twenty-one oil-fired which used creosote pitch oil fuel (would the latter fuel be accepted today?)

Many of the required forgings made originally by the blacksmith were increasingly being produced by steam-hammer die stamping or by the electrically powered drop hammer. In both cases, dependent on size, a facility for making 'die sinking' machine, a form of milling machine, which cut the die block to the required matching shapes. Also during the 1940s was installed a very large steam accumulator to supply the shop's steam requirements from a bank of boilers. Thus by the 1940s and 1950s much of traditional blacksmith work was done mechanically.

NO. 19A & 19B SHOPS – TRIMMING

In association with No. 9 Shop (page 137) and part of No. 9 Shop (19c Shop), the third in the group, No. 19 Shop, was for carriage lifting by the use of hydraulics, and the use of a special 'drop pit' arrangement. Instead of actually lifting the coach off its bogies, the coach is run over a specially designed pit which had tables onto which the coach was positioned. The tables could be lowered into the pit once the bogie had been freed and then run out of the pit literally underground. A reverse of the system accommodated the replacement bogies.

19D SHOP – CARRIAGE VACUUM BRAKE & BOGIE REPAIR

Here, mechanics paid special attention to axle boxes and spring suspension. The condition of wheels and bearings were checked and reconditioned as required.

NO. 20 SHOP – HORSE BOX & CARRIAGE TRUCK REPAIRS

This shop retained what could be called a 'historical' name. At this period the horsebox had a long design history from its original shape outlined in the opening chapters of this book, but was still very much valid. There could not have been very much work of the second type of repair mentioned. The carriage truck was more a historical relic, as how many families now travelled in their own road coaches with transport also required for horses and staff? No. 20 Shop was now relocated within the No. 21 Shop building (Wagon Repairs).

No. 18 Shop: dies for stamping draw-hook and spring buckle.

NO. 21 SHOP – WAGON BUILDING & REPAIRS

21 & 21b Wood Wagons – This was again a flow-type operation, receiving completed frames from No. 13 Shop for the many types of wood wagons such as covered goods, fruit vans, goods brake vans, sheep wagons, cattle wagons etc., with a flow-line for open wagon repairs. Repair lines operated through the length of the shop – in one end, out the other – well set out in this 700ft long x 150ft wide shop.

21a – was a 250ft x 150ft portioned-off side of the long Wood Repair Shop and was for iron wagon attention, with all the usual welding and riveting facilities.

21b – was the designated area for wagon painting, with stencilling and sign writing, numbers and letters, for identifying wagon notices for use and function, as well as any travelling restrictions.

NO. 22 – THE OIL & GREASE WORKS

Mentioned earlier was the fact that the Great Western at Swindon mixed or made, among many other requirements, its own oils and grease. Any mechanical item which is associated with friction, such as sliding or rotating surfaces subject to pressure from another surface will generate heat. This still occurs even if regularly and effectively lubricated, and if controlled by its

No. 18 Shop: hydraulic pressing of brackets, heated in the furnace on the left.

No. 19 Carriage Lifting Shop.

No. 19 Carriage Lifting Shop: bogie assembly.

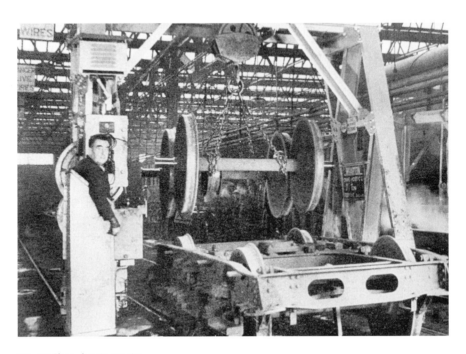

No. 19 Shop: bogie repairs.

No. 21 Shop: the wagon production line.

No. 24 Shop under construction, 1929. the cottage is the lock keeper's home on the now abandoned North Wilts Canal.

Timber Stores — No 21 Shop.

F3/227 19.6.35

No. 21 The New Shop: wagon repairs (wood).

Paint-mixing.

PAINT STORES - MANUFACTURE. F3·149 NEG.
TOP FLOOR - STOCK OF DRY COLOURS ZINC & OXIDE
PASTE LIQUIDS ETC. PHOTO 10.2

F3/294
25/7/50

Above: No. 22: oil-blending.

Opposite top: Paint Stores (manufacture) – top floor: stock of dry colours, zinc and oxide paste, and liquids.

Opposite bottom: No. 22 Shop: Oil Works.

Swindon Oil Stores

F3. 309
6.12.51

No. 22 Shop: Swindon Oil Stores.

No. 23 Shop: Carriage & Wagon Works Plate Layers' Yard.

constituents, designed for specific situations, can be beneficial in the action of the lubricant.

Incorrect or interrupted lubrication will cause excessive build–up of heat thus damaging the surfaces of whatever bearing is so affected.[1] With grease lubrication a certain amount of generated heat is required to bring out the best lubricating state of the grease. The major difference between axle boxes designed for grease and those designed for oil is in the 'feeding' of the lubricant to the journal. In the former it is fed in from the top section of the box and with the latter the feed is from underneath the journal, usually from a 'keep' containing a mop–like spring-loaded pad, such as an Armstrong oiler or a thick felt strip.

The bearing itself for a grease axle box is generally made from bronze consisting of approximately 88 per cent pure copper, 10 per cent tin and 2 per cent zinc, whilst the bearing for oil lubrication is a bronze with a bearing surface of white metal, which is applied in a molten state to the running pressure surface only and to which the preparation ensures adherence. The white metal bearing surface is fitted to the journal by scraping the high spots on the marked surface using 'engineers' blue'.

The constituents of general axle grease are:

1 not less than 10 per cent mineral oil
2 40 per cent (not more than) wood fat and soda soap
3 50 per cent water (surprising perhaps?)

It should be noted that modern–day bearings are usually roller or ball races, often grease packed for life! All bearings, particularly in the days of steam, were run–in comparatively slowly, to allow the bearing to bed-in on the journal.

Swindon's Oil & Grease Works was introduced during the 1880s, along with the expansion and building of greater capacity workshops for the building of wagons.

There are two buildings with the No. 22 Shop identification. In the early years, although lubrication was a recognised essential, engineers were very limited in what could be used. Vegetable, animal and fish oils were available for both lubrication and illumination. Melted tallow for the former and whale oil for the latter were among the very limited range available. All this changed in the 1880s when the benefits of newly discovered mineral oil were added to the range, in all its varied forms. Thus the first No. 22 Shop was classified as the Grease Works,

---

1. I remember from my apprentice days in Swindon's 'A' Erecting Shop, when a locomotive crank axle overheated and the bearing seized up completely, thus locking the journal to the axle box bearing. The locomotive travelling at speed had literally twisted the wheel off the axle, leaving the stub of the axle still securely keyed into the wheel, with the twisting action clear on the broken axle end.

with the Oil Works coming along years later (see the Works layout map for 1920 which indicates the addition of the Oil Works). By 1950 it was recorded that approximately 6,000 tons of lubricating oil and 460 tons of wagon axle grease were issued by No. 22 Shop each year, 2,900 tons allocated to the locomotives, with the remainder for the other rolling stock.

A small laboratory continued with analysis and experimentation of mixing and blending of oils, some from a recovery plant which cleaned the liquids for reuse and blending. A considerable amount of oil was salvaged in this way, passing through various filters etc., recorded at about 250 tons per year reblended for further use. The blending tanks feed to storage tanks which can store 400 tons of oil in the thirteen 10,000-gallon storage tanks.

There was also a dry cleaning facility for protective clothing and cloths beloved of the painters. The cleaning fluids were also collected, themselves cleaned and recycled.

NO. 23 SHOP – PLATE LAYERS' YARD

Not strictly a 'shop' as such but with a small building housing office and rest facilities, with an area for maintenance, salvaging and breaking-up of unwanted and items for scrap. Works 'plate laying' track maintenance as required, their general work listed as follows, a wide range of activities, in addition to the plate laying or track maintenance mentioned above, all in the Carriage & Wagon Works:

Lagging boilers and steam pipes with asbestos plaster;
Packing special vehicles;
Breaking condemned coaches and wagons;
Cleaning all drains, gutters, windows and roof glass in the Carriage & Wagon
    Works;
Loading all wagons with scrap metal;
Sweeping and cleaning yards and lavatories;
Laying 'Magnesite' flooring in new and repaired coaches;
Relaying concrete floors in the Carriage Works.

NO. 24 SHOP

Built in 1927, this shop was for carriage repairs and repainting, extending the work of No. 6 Shop in line with increases in traffic. The shop was 600ft long, covering about 7 acres in area. The flow-put included about 1,500 coaches, which required a heavy repair and a complete repaint. External repairs were carried out first, on examination by the foreman deciding what had to be done. Outer doors and fittings, panelling, mouldings etc. were checked and repairs undertaken as specified before the internal work was done. Eight roads in the shop were allocated for what could be called 'normal' repairs with a usual time of fourteen days allowed, extended when a heavy repair was required, particularly when the condition necessitated separating body and underframe when lifting was required – this undertaking, as outlined in the section on No. 19c Shop, was not really lifting as such.

No. 24c Shop Complex – these shops were built on an area of land acquired from the Local Authority at Swindon in exchange for what had been the Great Western Park, a recreation area with its own pavilion and bandstand, now both long gone, and the venue for the famed Great Western Fête, on entry to which children were presented with a large slab of specially made Great Western cake. Those were the days!

THE DE-INFESTATION PLANT

Adjacent to the new No. 24 Shop there was a long narrow building housing a steel cylinder 85ft x 16½ft in diameter, into which a rail line was continued. Coaches and any special wagons could be run-in and a sealing disc door could be slid into place which hermetically sealed the end. Special pumps and steam heating pipes could then be put into action, the pumps to create a partial vacuum to remove as much air as possible, and the steam pipes to raise the temperature to 49°C (or 120°F). This temperature was maintained for about six hours – although it is unlikely that this would kill all bugs. There was a further treatment, however, which could be applied to a carriage or wagon suspected of contact with a contaminated person or item, say a tropical disease, where a dose of formalin was introduced as the vacuum was reduced, thus creating formaldehyde and killing off the contaminant.

Of interest is the door-sealing ring, 16½ft in diameter, machined in the Locomotive Works 'G' (Millwrights) Shop. This was a job for the very skilled operator of this very old machine, to set up without distortion, on the lathe's 8ft-diameter faceplate, at least a quarter of the ring, and the lathe itself below ground level.

The workshop itself was an original from the opening of the complex, where it started life as the Boiler Shop, illustrated by Bourne in his 1845 range of prints.

Adjacent No. 24 Shop, the De-infestation Plant: Turning the ring seal.

AUTHOR'S NOTE – C. 1963

The transfer of the Carriage & Wagon remnants to the ex-locomotive workshops – around 1963, when I was area assistant for the South West – involved me in a number of episodes. One incident I remember, in particular, concerned wagon repairs, which were to continue and so the hunt was on for a suitable workshop. I looked at the shops becoming available, and decided that the L2 Steam Loco Tender Repair Shop would be ideal, as it had a multi-rail outside yard which continued inside the shop and easy access to and from the shop – an essential requirement for the job! So, having prepared a drawing with internal shop proposed additions, I sat back awaiting the call from the chief.

Before the call came, I received a drawing to vet which proposed using the Boiler Shop (the 'V' Shop) for wagon repairs. The traversing table outside and between the L2 Shop and the 'V' Shop had by now been scrapped and the only access to the Boiler Shop was one rail track past one end, along the road outside the 'V' Shop and the end blanked off by the 'W' Shop. On the drawing it seemed everywhere there appeared a little turntable, outside to get into the shop through 90° and within the shop to get onto the right rail tracks.

I considered this completely impractical and said so in the report I forwarded as requested, also forwarding my own report and drawing of the L2 Shop. I did not hear anything in return and the next thing I discovered was the alterations rapidly under way with the little turntables and the 'V' Shop layout.

What I didn't know at the time was that the 'V' Shop design and proposal was by the chief himself, Mr Scott, the CME. So, a fait accompli!

This period was the beginning of the end of the complete Works – the work quantity becoming less and less and seemingly more trivial. Staff numbers continually reduced and the Works closed in 1986. The site is now home to a shopping mall as well as STEAM, the museum of the GWR.

APPENDIX A

THE QUEST FOR EFFICIENT BRAKES AND A SAFE SYSTEM OF APPLYING THEM

The brakes on carriages and wagons are inextricably linked to their 'power source': the motive power locomotive. How this source of brake power was applied, how the number of individual systems evolved, and the variation by numerous inventors and engineers in what developed into a competition, has been detailed in my previous book *The Steam Locomotive: An Engineering History*. Thus, this section has been taken in entirety for inclusion in this book, as it answers the question of Great Western's rolling stock brake development.

★　★　★

From quite early on in the locomotive's development, attempts at safe and effective braking are well documented. The number of trains continued to grow, speeds generally were increasing (it took a number of years for other companies to match the Great Western broad gauge in this respect) and with these increases, so increased the number of accidents. There were numerous attempts to devise a satisfactory brake system which could be applied to the complete train, not just selected brake-fitted vehicles – often only on one side of the tender – and a whistle-signalled application of a handbrake by the guard.

Increasingly heavier trains were being introduced, and among the many problems to be countered was that of a heavily laden train breaking in two when a coupling failed. Thus, came the compulsory 'fail-safe' requirement of brake application in the event that the train should separate. The field of experimentation was blown wide open. Theories were expounded, inventors burned the midnight oil, and proposals started to roll in, all awaiting the chance to prove themselves.

The quest for what is termed 'continuous braking' started in earnest at the turn of the mid-nineteenth century. In 1857 a patent obtained by a James Harris introduced one of the main braking power sources, compressed air. In principle a steam-driven compressor supplied air to receivers or tanks under each carriage and releasing the air applied a braking force. This was one of those patents where someone patents an idea or proposal and looks in vain for a producer.

There were really four methods of powering a braking system at this period: a straightforward steam brake which of necessity was eventually restricted to the locomotive itself; the use of compressed air or conversely the application of a vacuum operation; and finally, some form of hydraulic appliance all of which found advocates as designs proliferated. A possible fifth method was some form of manual application, which was really not practical.

In 1860, Du Trembly and Martin patented a vacuum application, whereby the system continues through metal pipework with a flexible connection between each coach – a procedure we recognise today. This proposal remained a proposal only, but carried the potential for future development. A crude steam application created a partial vacuum to collapse the flexible end or sac of the brake cylinders, thus applying the brakes.

The whole potential of compressed air and of vacuum application was recognised and triggered the design and development of the two important 'power' source mechanisms. In one case the steam operated air compressor – a piston compressor which, while it worked, was later developed for general engineering use into the much more efficient vane compressor. On the vacuum front the requirement for an effective 'ejector' to create and maintain the necessary vacuum. The vacuum pump, which in modern times maintains a vacuum, came along considerably later, but in the early years a 'pump' of sorts, competed with the 'exhauster', itself a forerunner of the ejector.

Prior to these power applications, a proposal which was actually fitted to a train was that of D. Clark around 1870. This comprised a system of levers each with a mechanical advantage when operated by a lowered weight attached to a chain, which ran centrally along the complete length of the train.

Joined by links at each coach, the supporting pulleys also had the effect of increasing the pull on brake blocks of cast iron swinging on hangers on each side of each wheel. In tests, a 90-ton train, not including the engine, was stopped in 245 yards from running at 55mph on a 1 in 99 gradient. The period six-wheel coaches could be fitted with the system at a cost of £17 each. Whilst moderately successful it did not really catch on.

A proposal by the same railway engineer utilised hydraulic power to operate the braking system. With this idea a 1½in pipe always filled with water, ran the length of the train, flexible couplings joining the individual carriage pipes. Each coach was fitted with a 6in cylinder, its piston attached to a lever on a shaft, which, by other levers, pulled the brake blocks onto the wheels. Power was supplied by steam to the piston in a 'charging chamber' on the engine. This force compressed the water in the system and applied the brakes, the water incidentally being mixed with an anti-freeze solution. Again this system worked.

There were, of course, worldwide attempts to solve the braking problem of trains which increasingly were getting bigger and heavier. An example from the Great Indian Peninsula Railway utilised a vacuum to keep the brakes in the 'off' position. Breaking the vacuum allowed the spring-loaded brake gear to clamp around the wheels. This system also had a built-in safety arrangement, in that in the event of a train breaking in two through a failed coupling the destroyed vacuum automatically applied the brakes.

There were many early contenders for the continuous-brake development crown, but two suggestions, in particular, came to the fore. These were the vacuum system and the application of compressed air. Among the names of the vacuum proponents we find those of Smith, Sanders and Westinghouse, all successful in their own way. Westinghouse was to leave the vacuum contenders and concentrate on the compressed air version, which had had great success to the extent of replacing Loughbridge's air brake, then widely used on the railroads of America.

Such competition and variations of proposals and applications led inevitably to a requirement of a joint discussion between government and engineers to review the situation and come up with a proposal for standardisation on all Britain's railways. Stemming from the talks came a proposal for a series of practical trials. Although at this period it was thought essential for a brake to be fitted to the tender and the rest of the train, whatever its length, the locomotive itself was not considered at all – it being thought that reversing the valve gear and opening the regulator would suffice (I have very strong reservations on the use of such tactics unless in an acute emergency as such activity does not do the valve gear or other components any good at all!)

The effectiveness of the vacuum system was given a great boost when, in 1877, Graham obtained his first of many allied patents and introduced the first practical 'ejector'. Although mention was made earlier that a brake on the locomotive itself was not really necessary, there were other engineers with more practical ideas. A locomotive running light needs better stopping power than a hand-screwed tender brake. Many engines of the period were already fitted with a steam brake devised by Roberts and later incorporating McConnell's improvements. On the Continent, Chatelier's counter-pressure brake had also been in service for some time.

There were set out in the brake trial requirements papers eighteen specific essentials for a practical and acceptable continuous-brake system. These, in brief, were that the brake had to be in charge of, and easily operated by, the driver. Action should be controllable from partial to full application depending on requirements for such application. It should be simple to maintain. If one portion of the system failed it should not affect the rest of the system regarding brake application. Vehicles making up a train may be various and must not affect coupling-up or braking. Any length of train was to be braked with uniform efficiency. Brake blocks should apply, and thus wear evenly, without undue wear on any part of the wheel tyre. Brakes to remain 'on' when applied but capable of instant release when required. As a safety measure, access to operation by the passengers must not affect the overall safety of the train.

In retrospect, it is surprising to find that compensation payments in the non-braked or experimental years were reaching very high figures. For example, the year 1872–73 saw payments of £311,000 in compensation alone, whilst damage to rolling stock reached the astonishing figure of £650,000. Something obviously had to be done! The railway companies involved included the Caledonian, Great Northern, London Brighton & South Coast, London & North Western, Lancashire & Yorkshire, Midland and the North Eastern. With their approval, the Midland had placed a suitable length of track between Newark and Thurgarton on the Nottingham to Lincoln branch at the disposal of the Government Brake Commission. The braking systems to be tried out comprised Barker's hydraulic, Clark's chain, Clark's hydraulic, Fay's handbrake, Smith's vacuum, Steel-McInnes' reaction airbrake, Westinghouse's automatic compressed air and Westinghouse's vacuum. The trials got under way, purposes progressed satisfactorily, with all test requirements being covered. At the end of the day however, it was clear that no decisions or selection of any of the systems had been made, the onus being put back on the designers to 'acquire additional brake power in what way seemed best to them'.

As with all experimental work, some designs seemingly based on a good idea inevitably proved impractical when applied in practice. One such design which had the brake blocks applied to the rail and not the wheel was that known as the 'sledge brake'. If applied with force, the blocks had the effect of lifting the wagon bodily off the rails, particularly if running light.

So, what had been termed the 'Battle of the Brake' continued and, in 1878, the Institution of Mechanical Engineers sought to end the confusion by appointing a Captain Douglas Galton to undertake another series of tests. Whilst the first trials, inconclusive as they were, had examined the practical uses of the systems, these trials had a more scientific approach to include determining the coefficient of friction between brake blocks and wheels, and between rails and wheels, strains on the engine drawbar and the time constraints of initiating and completing brake application. Coefficients of adhesion between wheel and rail related to speed; brake block pressures on the wheels were also subjects of Galton's study.

These intensive studies followed by experiments and modifications, shown to be required to approach something like the requirements of the perfect brake, only led to a checkmate. The several parties with interests in a particular system had by now got the message that their system was now on a par with several others. No 'standard' selection could thus be made, and individual railways were left to their own choice, as long as that choice fulfilled the criteria for safe braking.

An 1859 Act of Parliament required all trains carrying passengers to be fitted with automatic power brakes. The Railway Act of 1921, bringing all companies (with one or two exceptions) into the 'Big Four' net has generally endorsed the vacuum automatic brake as the standard for British steam trains. The perfection of the vacuum brake thus virtually achieved has led to quite complex, but easily operated, designs some incorporating joint application of the locomotive steam brake and the train vacuum system through the operation of a simple lever operated valve – a long struggle which paid off in the end.

The design of the brake isn't everything. You have to know when to apply them. In the years prior to this book the railway system had suffered some horrendous crashes, signals not seen, not acted upon etc. This was followed by a rush for some magical electronic device to solve the problem. The Great Western had this wrapped up eighty years ago! The following page tells the story, proudly presented for the Great Western Centenary in 1935.

THE QUEST FOR EFFICIENT BRAKES
(And How To Control Them)

THE GREAT WESTERN WAY: AUTOMATIC TRAIN CONTROL (ATC)

Safety of travel on the G.W.R. has been much enhanced by the adoption of a system of automatic train control by means of which audible warning is given to the enginemen of the condition of distant signals, and in the event of one being passed at "caution" the train is stopped automatically before it reaches the next signal. There is a steel ramp, 40 ft. long and rising to $3\frac{1}{4}$ in. above rail level, midway in the four-foot opposite the distant signal, and connected to the signal lever electrically. When the signal is at "caution" the ramp is dead; the action of pulling the lever to give a "clear" indication of the distant signal completes an electric circuit and energises the ramp. On the locomotive is fitted an iron shoe, with a T-shaped end extending head downwards to within $2\frac{1}{4}$ in. of rail level. As the engine passes over the ramp the head of the T comes into contact with it and is lifted 1 in. If the signal is at "caution" the ramp is dead, and the action of lifting the shoe opens a valve on the vacuum-automatic brake apparatus and causes the brakes to be applied throughout the train, at the same time sounding a siren in the engine cab. If the signal is in the "clear" position, the ramp is energised and the electric current, passing through the shoe, prevents interference with the vacuum brake, but rings an electric bell in the engine cab. This type of signal was first introduced on the Henley branch in January, 1906, and on the Fairford branch in December of the same year. By September, 1931, the whole of the Great Western Railway main lines, totalling 2,130 miles had been equipped, as well, of course, as all the locomotives liable to work over these lines.

Engine approaching A.T.C. ramp on a typical section of G.W.R. standard track

The shoe fixture under the front of the locomotive – The hardened shoe is spring loaded and the 'lift' is about 1in.

The bell/siren equipment at the right-hand side of the cab.

THE AIR BRAKE

The Great Western's *King George V*: Fitted with an air pump on a test run prior to the visit to the Baltimore & Ohio Railway centenary exhibition in 1928. (The famous bell was presented at the exhibition.) The air pump was designed to match the common American braking system.

Eight-wheeled 'American' locomotive by The Hinkley Locomotive Company, Boston, Mass. An American locomotive of *c*. 1890 fitted with the Westinghouse air brake system. There were also several vacuum brake systems, but mostly air brakes were used.

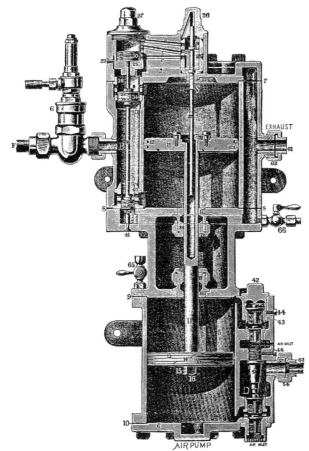

Brake air pump.

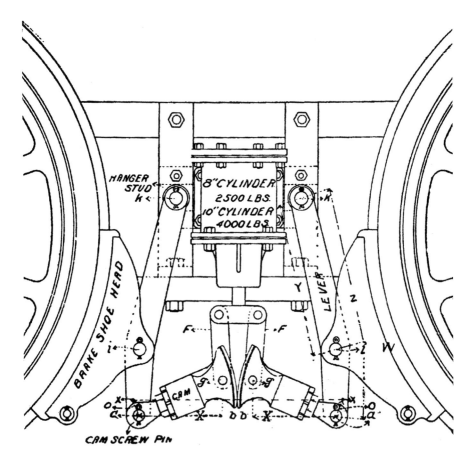

Driving wheel brake: there was one of these arrangements on both sides of the locomotive.

THE GREAT WESTERN WAY – AUTOMATIC TRAIN CONTROL (ATC) 1931

Safety of travel on the GWR has been much enhanced by the adoption of a system of automatic train control by means of which audible warning is given to the enginemen of the condition of distant signals, and in the event of one being passed at 'caution' the train is stopped automatically before it reaches the next signal. There is a steel ramp, 40ft long and rising to 3½in above rail level, midway in the 4ft opposite the distant signal, and connected to the signal lever electrically. When the signal is at 'caution' the ramp is dead; the action of pulling the lever to give a 'clear' indication of the distant signal completes an electric circuit and energises the ramp. On the locomotive is fitted an iron shoe, with a T-shaped end extending head downwards to within 2½in of rail level. As the engine passes over the ramp the head of the 'T' comes into contact with it and is lifted 1in. If the signal is at 'caution' the ramp is dead, and the action of lifting the shoe opens a valve on the vacuum-automatic brake apparatus and causes the brakes to be applied throughout the train, at the same time sounding a siren in the engine cab. If the signal is in the 'clear' position, the ramp is energised and the electric current, passing through the shoe, prevents interference with the vacuum brake, but rings an electric bell in the engine cab. This type of signal was first introduced on the Henley branch in January 1906 and on the Fairford branch in December of the same year. By September 1931 the whole of Great Western Railway main lines, totalling 2,130 miles, had been equipped – as well of course as all the locomotives liable to work over these lines.

COMPONENTS OF THE VACUUM BRAKE SYSTEM

The 'ejector': This works in a way similar to the boiler feed 'injector', with steam passing through a series of cone exhausts, thus removing the air from the vacuum system. The 'injector', through a series of cones, forces water into the boiler.

The 'vacuum pump': Stops the use of steam when the loco is moving by taking over from the ejector, being operated mechanically by the movement of the loco – crosshead thus economising on the use of steam.

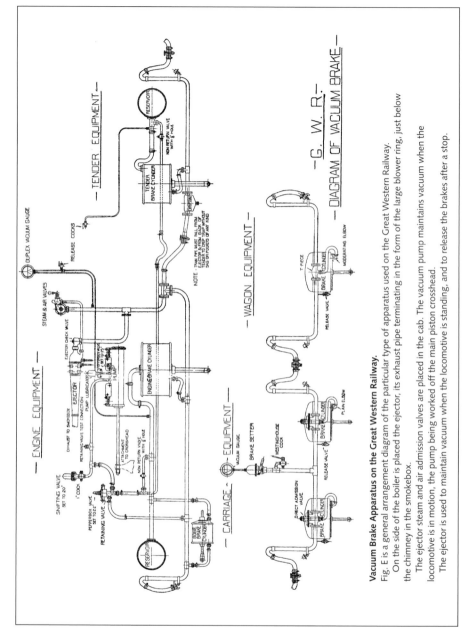

Vacuum Brake Apparatus on the Great Western Railway.

Fig. E is a general arrangement diagram of the particular type of apparatus used on the Great Western Railway.

On the side of the boiler is placed the ejector; its exhaust pipe terminating in the form of the large blower ring, just below the chimney in the smokebox.

The ejector steam and air admission valves are placed in the cab. The vacuum pump maintains vacuum when the locomotive is in motion, the pump being worked off the main piston crosshead.

The ejector is used to maintain vacuum when the locomotive is standing, and to release the brakes after a stop.

The complete system fitted to the locomotive and tender. The right-hand group (tender) also under carriages and wagons.

The arrangement of Vacuum Brakes on carriages and wagons. A and B represent those used by GWR, while C and D are examples of alternative types.

Vacuum Brake Locomotive Type.

This type of cylinder is shown at Fig. A.

The top and bottom covers of these cylinders are separate from the cylinder barrel, the covers being fixed to the barrel by means of separate bolts which extend the length of the barrel.

The engine cylinder has a bore diameter of 30in, and the tender cylinder a diameter of 22in. The engine cylinders are usually placed either under the footplate of the cab or about midway between the smokebox and the firebox and between the engine frames.

The pistons are fitted with rubber bands similar to those of the rolling stock type.

A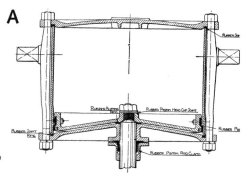

Vacuum Cylinders. Rolling Stock Type.

This type of cylinder is shown in Fig. B.

The piston head, instead of having the usual rolling ring, is fitted with a rubber band (2½in wide by 5/16in thick), the outer half of this band is impregnated with graphite, so as to reduce friction between the cylinder wall and the rubber to a minimum. The upper portion of the band is clipped firmly to the piston head by means of a thin steel clip, the head being treated with rubber solution before the band is fitted. These bands give roughly about two years continuous service.

Air is drawn from the top or chamber side of the piston past this band, hence there is no need for a valve either at the elbow connection of the cylinder or in the piston head, though for releasing the brakes by hand, a release valve is fitted to the side of the carriage and wagon cylinders, so as to admit air to the chamber when necessary.

B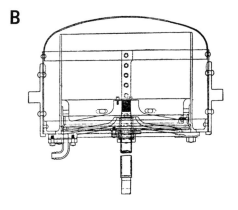

Combined Cylinder. (Pressed steel).

Fig. C illustrated the latest type of 'Prestall' combined cylinder in which, 1 is the chamber and 2 the cylinder barrel. These are electrically welded at their lowest extremities to a substantial foundation ring. The construction of the base and piston head is the same as that of the separate type. The base, however, is secured to the chamber foundation ring by means of studs, which do not screw through the ring as with the type in which it is obvious that the studs are liable to permit of leakage past the threads into the chamber.

C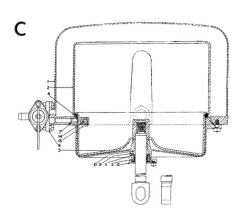

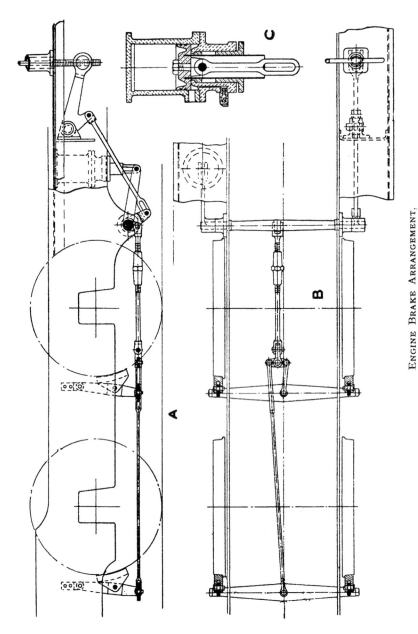

Engine Brake Arrangement.

Steam/hand brake combination (independent use). Illustrated are rods and shafts, and a sectioned steam cylinder: the latter is a simple brake arrangement to have complete safety when moving just the locomotive without preparing the vacuum system.

Controlled braking attempts: Moving into the twentieth century, loads for both carriages and wagons were getting bigger and heavier as the century evolved, thus the transport involved had to follow suit in design. Braking had always been a problem; a very heavily loaded wagon takes more braking power to stop than it does when empty, so schemes evolved to enable variable braking pressures to be applied to suit the load. Some were unsuccessful but two of the better ideas are shown on this page. A variable braking system devised by Messrs Gresham & Craven are shown with the two cylinder version, whilst 'clasp' braking, with brake blocks gripping both sides of the wheel was successfully tried, although in example C it gave consistent braking power which was not selective for any load, but more power than one block. (Examples from the 1930s and '40s.)

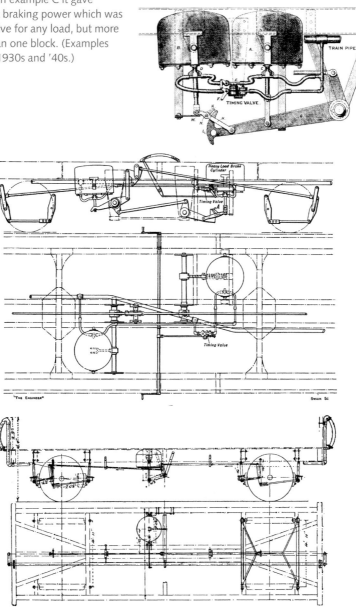

APPENDIX B

A NOTE ON WELDING

THE REVOLUTION IN REPAIR AND CONSTRUCTION

The art of joining metals has been known and practised for hundreds of years. Forms of brazing and soldering have been found on many items exhibiting different shapes of differing metals being attached to a main item, such as copper wires in patterns decorating a dagger sheath found at a Bronze Age grave site.

The main iron joining method, also known for hundreds of years, is part and parcel of the work of the blacksmith. The sparkling white-hot length of iron bar attached by hammer blows to an iron bar in similar condition and forming a permanent join is something with which we are all familiar.

The discovery of a method of making electric power, and its continuing experimental use resulted in lighting far stronger that of the early nineteenth-century's existing candles and oil (not forgetting the carbide lamps made from about 1800 onwards, after acetylene gas, which led again to an interesting side shoot of discovery). The piercing light from the ends of two carbon rods connected to two wires, positive and negative, when held in proximity to each other but not touching gave us the arc lamp from which it was found the light also was associated with heat. Could this heat be used for some other application?

Experimenting continued and, as with other discoveries, several experimenters came up with the same answer around the same time, two of them being one Russian (Bernardo) and one American (Coffin) who came up with carbon-arc welding, around the first half of the 1880s. A development around 1890 produced the technique of bare-wire welding, again developed by a Russian (Slavianor) and the American, Coffin. Also during this period Henry Howard brought the carbon-arc process to Britain from Russia (Howard founded the steel firm Stewarts & Lloyds). During 1902, Dr Carl von Linde had found a way of producing cheap oxygen and in only a matter of a couple of years the combination of oxygen and acetylene produced a controllable heat source.

Oxygen itself had been discovered by Priestley in England, and Scheele in Sweden, as early as c. 1774 and Humphry Davy had applied acetylene for lamps in 1800 but it was to be many years before a successful combination of the two was found to be a useful source of heat for welding and conversely flame cutting

– this around 1905. This success was only possible because of the successful design of a gas-combining hand-held torch. An early attempt by Thomas Fletcher had produced a blowpipe in 1887 and this had been using a combination of hydrogen or coal gas with oxygen. Reputedly among its first successful uses was by safe crackers for opening bank safes. Not an auspicious introduction! But the improvements in 1903 by Fouche and Piccard produced a reliable mixer torch for oxy-acetylene welding and cutting.

Experiments with aluminium powder and metal oxides from the 1850s showed what at the time was an unexploited welding potential and it took nearly fifty years for Dr Hans Goldschmidt to prove that the early process worked well when iron oxides were mixed with aluminium powder and heat was applied. This became known as 'thermit' welding, a demonstration of which I remember watching as an apprentice, when a piece of railway line was inserted into a short very damaged section effecting a rapid, and what appeared to be a dangerous, procedure! There was an almost immediate joint, which was afterwards ground off to restore the profile.

However, going back to the early 1800s, Humphry Davy had also carried out carbon rod experiments with Volta's battery, but this was restricted to the production of a consistent and dependable source of light and not heat. Several experimenters early in the nineteenth century had experimented with the carbon arc, and as early as 1849 W.E. Staite obtained a patent for electric arc welding, purely on an experimental basis. Both lighting and welding had to wait for the development of a generator before becoming practical, although the dynamo by Wilde, and the ring dynamo by Gramme in 1871 worked quite well, until arc lighting was overtaken by the Swan and Edison successes with the filament lamp around 1878 – later to be exploited for railway carriage lighting.

Bare-wire welding included a separately held wire to be combined with the arc heat. Around 1910, Kjell of Sweden developed the coated electrode, whilst in Britain Strohmenger developed the quasi-arc electrode, which was wrapped in asbestos yarn, the function of a carbon rod now taken over by the electrode. The wrapped electrode, with continually developing coatings and their application, is one with which we are all familiar. Their application and development continued apace, leading to the combination of the arc and gas in such applications as argon arc welding, the gas preserving the integrity of the weld deposit from impurities of combustion.

Early welding appeared to be restricted to repairs as construction methods still utilised the riveted joint for all new work. The exigencies of the First World War, however, changed all that as speed became the essence. The rivet was considered a labour intensive application and, at a time when the labour market was low because of the requirements of the armed services, quicker alternatives were sought. Riveting began to fade out as new techniques of welding took over, being applied to more and more engineering projects until complete ships were constructed solely by welding. Railway construction did not escape, with locomotive boilers both repaired and fully constructed by welding, as well as carriage and wagon frames and components clamped then welded into place; this was clean, rapid work. The developments in spot welding were applied throughout the car industry.

Modern, huge spherical pressure vessels for application even to nuclear submarines were all completely welded. Apart from 'heritage' type repairs for current engineering projects, the rivet is now itself a historical relic, rarely used except to preserve historical accuracy.

Development, once it started, was very fast, the variations in types of welding up to approximately the twentieth century are listed below:

Arc Welding & Cutting

Carbon Arc Welding

Plug Welding

Arc Cutting and Piercing

Metal Arc Welding

Metal Arc Welding (Coated Electrodes)

Gas Welding & Cutting

Oxy-Acetylene Welding

Oxy-Acetylene/Gas Cutting

Resistance Welding

Butt Welding

Spot Welding

Seam Welding (Pipes etc)

Projection Welding

Flash Butt Welding

Other Methods

'Thermit' Welding

Plasma Cutting

Laser Cutting

Later, twentieth-century techniques include: friction welding and electron beam welding (c. 1961), multi-wire submerged arc welding, gas-shielded cored wire welding and explosive welding. Iron powder electrodes have even been used. Development never stops!

It must be emphasised that welding is not as straightforward as it sounds! Great care must be exercised in selecting the correct electrode for the job as well as setting the correct amperage. For in all welded structures, frames, bogies etc., if not applied in the correct sequence, the deposited weld material can make the component twist all over the place due to the uneven heating of the components to be welded. Secure clamping of components is often essential, with time to cool before release.

APPENDIX C

OTHER GREAT WESTERN SITES OF CARRIAGE & WAGON WORKS

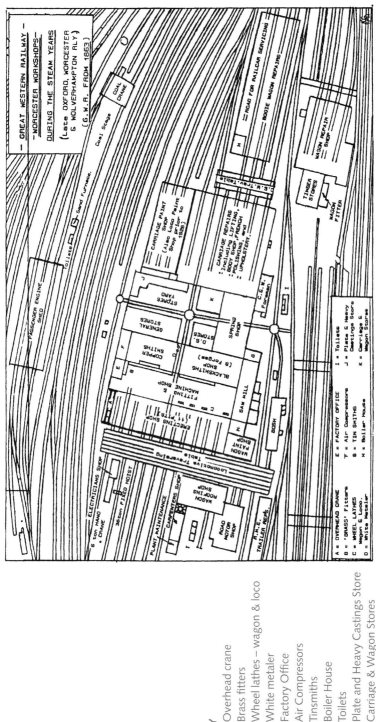

The GWR Worcester Workshops during the steam years (late Oxford, Worcester & Wolverhampton Railway, which became GWR in 1863).

KEY

A Overhead crane
B Brass fitters
C Wheel lathes – wagon & loco
D White metaler
E Factory Office
F Air Compressors
G Tinsmiths
H Boiler House
I Toilets
J Plate and Heavy Castings Store
K Carriage & Wagon Stores

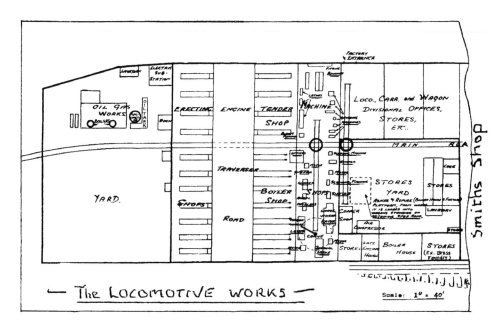

GWR Locomotive: Carriage & Wagon Works, Oswestry, 1937 (Originally the workshops of the Cambrian Railway).

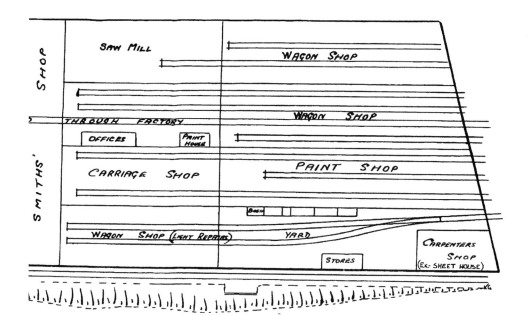

Cambrian Railway Works, Oswestry: the Carriage & Wagon Works.

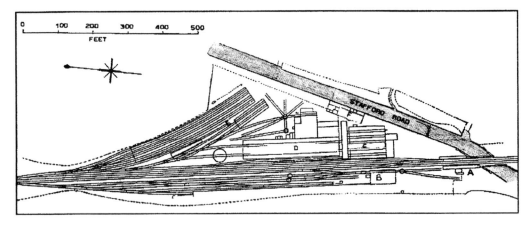

The Stafford Road headquarters of the Shrewsbury & Birmingham Railway c. 1849.

KEY

A   Passenger stations and platforms (temporary)
B   Goods station & yard (temporary)
C   Repair Shop and Traversing Table
D   Locomotive shed
E   Carriage & Wagon sheds
F   Offices

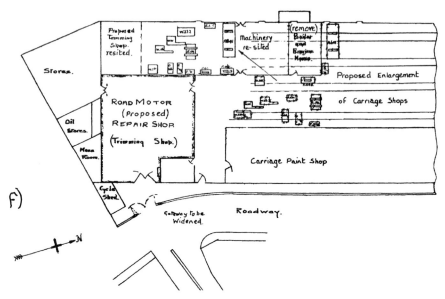

Newton Abbot: Proposed addition (8 November 1928). Although not a locomotive workshop, this drawing indicated the increasing influence of road motor transport on the railway system. (This development was in the Wagon & Carriage section of the Works, not shown on the other Newton Abbot plans.)

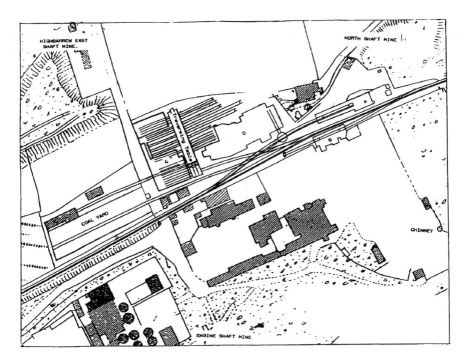

The GWR workshops at Carn Brea c. 1880, originally the shops of the Hayle Railway (1834), absorbed by the West Cornwall Railway (1846) and by GWR (1876). By 1880 it was in use as a carriage works which closed in 1917.

KEY
A Old broad-gauge (now mixed-gauge) loco shed
B Standard-gauge shed
C Carriage Shops
D Stores, Fitting and Machine Shops

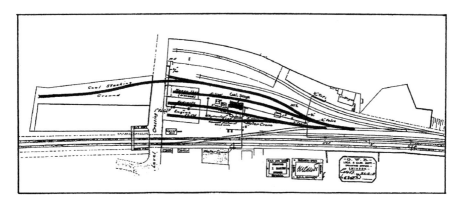

GWR Carn Brea Yard 1918.

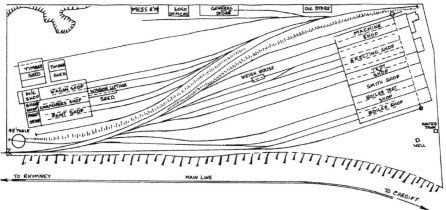

The Rhymney Railway Works at Caerphilly before development.

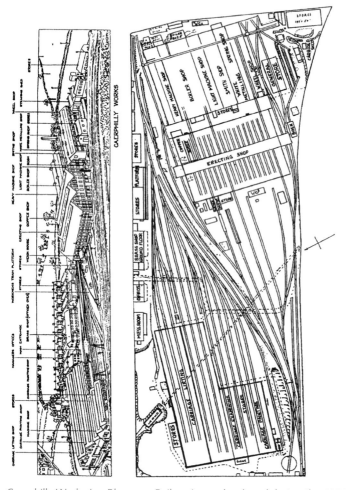

Caerphilly Works (ex-Rhymney Railway) as redeveloped during the 1920s.

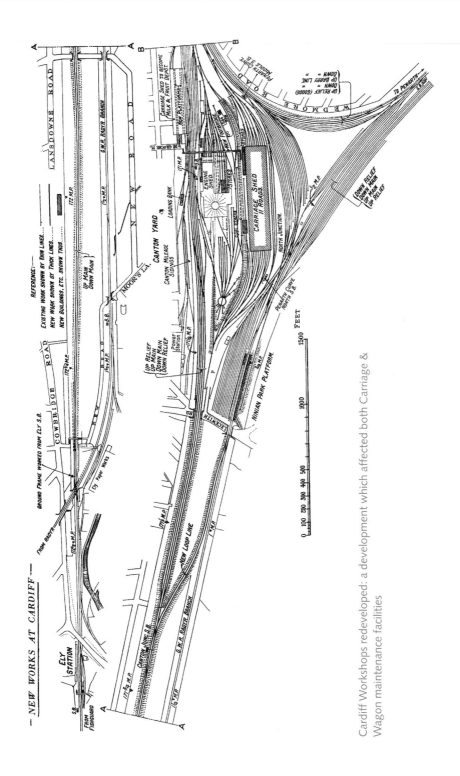

Cardiff Workshops redeveloped: a development which affected both Carriage & Wagon maintenance facilities

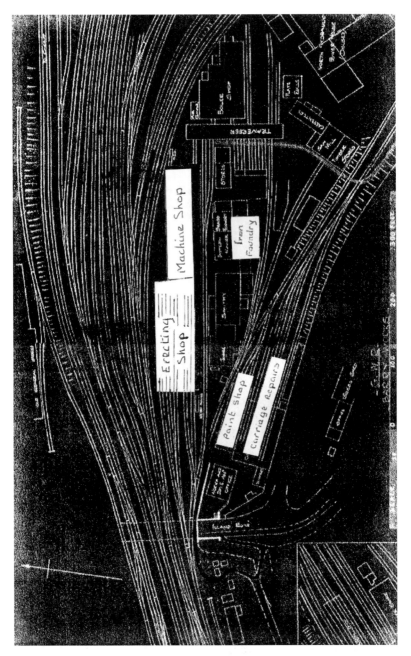

Great Western Railway: Barry Workshops (late Barry Dock & Railway Co. – Flatland Washes Railway from 1922).

The Bristol & Exeter Railway workshops of Bristol (Bath Rd), 1884. Originally opened in around 1851, they were extended by the Bristol & Exeter in 1854 and enlarged by the Great Western after takeover in 1876. They were completely demolished, redesigned and rebuilt in 1929–34.

Key

A	Cool stage.
B	Broad-gauge shed. Note mixed- & broad-gauged track.
C	Standard-gauge running shed of 1877 with 2 x 45ft turntables.
D	Workshop. Note that there are four rails instead of the usual three for mixed track. It ensured that the inspection pits were central under both broad- and standard-gauge locomotives.
E	Broad-gauge carriage shop.
F1, F2	Goods sheds inward & outward goods.
G1	Gitting & heavy machine shop.
G	Fitting & machine shop.
H	Weighbridge.
I	Smiths' shop.
J	Carpenters' shop.
K	Offices.
L	Original broad-gauge workshops (1851).

The 1892 Bristol avoiding line entailed demolition of half of the workshop building. Part of Sections I, and G, all of G1 and M were levelled.

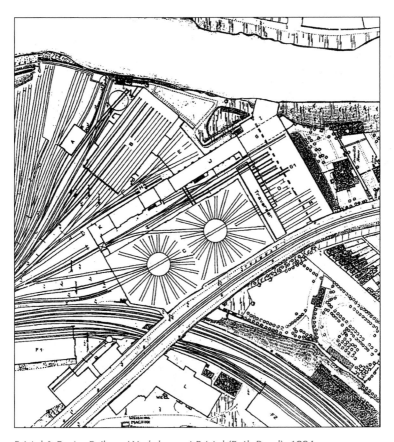

Bristol & Exeter Railway Workshops at Bristol (Bath Road), 1884.

APPENDIX D

A CARRIAGE SALVAGED!

The GWR, as it developed and spread had absorbed, by the 1930s, the astonishing figure of 353 railway companies (see my other book *The Great Western Railway: How It Grew*). These companies were either expanded, developed, or put out of business by the GWR; the last batch included in the amalgamation of the 1920s, which formed the 'Big Four', wasthe GWR, LMS, LNER and the SR.

Among those absorbed was the Cambrian (1922) which was itself a hybrid, being a varied-gauge combination of a number of separate railway companies, one of the bigger of eighteen with 104 locos and associated rolling stock in the 1922 group. The Great Western had, by 1922, already absorbed any company considered a commercial or financial threat, and the 1922 batch were taken over, including the Cambrian, following government directive, with of course a batch of odd and distinctive rolling stock, some of which could be Great Westernised or was alternatively selected for sale or scrapped, and which the GWR could well have done without in the first place. There was also a sale value in some of those destined to be scrapped. These could have the chassis separated from the carriage body for use for possibly a storage container or flat goods vehicle, while the stripped out body could become a shed for the garden or a house for chickens! A further use for those in better state were sold to become part of a dwelling – a very cheap way of arranging for someone to live in their own home.

There are now a surprising number of various carriage bodies still built into individual bungalows and being lived in, or as holiday lets, including some which were from the 1890s programme of scrapping the broad gauge, those designs which were pure broad gauge, and not designed for conversion to standard 4ft 8½in gauge, which were also eventually sold off. Some of those existing are probably now hidden by other structures as the family in residence naturally expanded and before the now existing very tight building regulations, where such use would probably now not be accepted.

Such a coach came to the attention of Nick Bailey of the Swindon & Cricklade Railway (which is rapidly developing, over the old track bed of the Midland South Western Junction Railway). The carriage is a hidden Cambrian Railway relic, mostly covered by various greenery and obscured by the other additional built-on structures, and dates from sometime around the 1890s. Upon examination the buried coach was identified as having been a six-wheeler first/second class combination, with a luggage compartment at one end, separate toilet facilities for the two classes which met at the coach centre and originally having upholstery of different patterns suitably distinguishing the differences between the two classes! Over the years, the four- and six-wheeled coaches, depending on condition, were being phased out, the current example being a 35ft version, now classed as very small when judged by the rapid coach developments, going up to virtually double that length.

As the bungalow in which it now sat was awaiting demolition, having been empty for several years, deterioration had set in and arrangements had to be rapidly made for its removal. This was organised, along with transport to its new site on the Swindon & Cricklade Railway. Accommodation for such a vehicle on any heritage site always proves difficult, but was solved surprisingly cheaply by housing it in a polytunnel as used for agriculture. This proved very effective; the tunnel had a few roof patches but has remained stable and weatherproof for several years, certainly keeping everything nicely dry.

The Cambrian carriage is accompanied in the polytunnel by a second rescued coach body from the North London Railway, now an empty shell sourced from a derelict bungalow like the Cambrian, but in better condition – in one end there

A model of a Cambrian coach – six-wheel version.

The Cambrian Coach: All shrubbery removed awaiting transport.

The Cambrian Coach at the start of its journey to Swindon & Cricklade Railway.

ILLUSTRATIONS FROM THE REBUILD RECORDS COMPILED BY CHRIS RANDALL (1894)

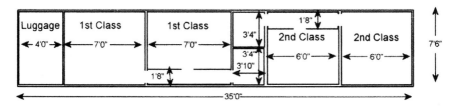

At 35ft overall length, No. 110 was amongst the longest (and last) six-wheel carriages built.

No. 110 early in 2011, after arriving at the Swindon & Cricklade Railway and being placed under the protection of a large horticultural polytunnel.

The underframe members were also repaired or renewed. Body-frame members were also repaired including a section of cant rail. All dry and wet rot are now gone – as well as the roof!

March 2012 saw all the main internal compartments erected, in conjunction with new roof hoops. As originally built, these are a mixture of wood and steel. For the first, we were working within the internal arrangements of the coach 'as built'. We were then in a position to reconstruct the corridor walls and the seat bases.

On 9 October 2013 the repanelling of one side of No. 110 was completed. Members of the team (not all present) allowed themselves a small celebration.

Earlier in March 2014 all the luggage compartment doors were permanently re-hung, with the original top/bottom bolts in place and working. Re-hanging all the external doors is an ongoing project at the time of writing.

With basic panelling complete on one side, progress is being made with producing the external mouldings. Here, a section is being test-fitted, June 2014.

205

remains wallpaper of Little Bo Peep, obviously part of a child's room. This one houses woodworking machinery and wood stocks, whilst work is concentrated on the Cambrian, which started as an empty shell, and which, due to rot removal, finished with no roof and requiring a new floor and side panelling. The frame condition was good.

Progression through the repairs to the body to date is shown by the accompanying photographs. The work required obtaining a suitable six-wheeled chassis or sufficient wheel sets to convert a four-wheel chassis to a six. Whatever wheel sets are acquired, they need altering by mock-up conversion to appear like the Mansell wood-centre originals!

The polytunnel has proved an excellent all weather protection giving access for working down a wide centre gangway and easy access round the other sides, ends and roof of both vehicles, the Cambrian being 35ft long and the North London Railway carriage about 30ft. With the latter, the end space makes a useful sales area for books, CDs, DVDs etc. in order to raise cash for the project, on which a regular group of six or seven work on the Cambrian – some members twice a week, some members also working at home during the week, all being retired officially with the addition of one rehabilitating injured military and one still serving Air Force personnel, both of great assistance and a most welcome addition to the group. We press on toward inclusion of one or both finished carriages as part of the Vintage Train Project.

If you enjoyed this book, you may also be interested in...

The Steam Workshops of the Great Western Railway

KEN GIBBS

978 0 7509 5912 4

The nineteenth century was a time of innovation and expansion across the industrial landscape, and nowhere more so than on the railways, as the new age of iron, steel and steam literally gathered pace. At the head of the race up was the iconic Great Western Railway. As this mighty corporation grew, it absorbed an astonishing 353 railway companies. Many of them had their own workshops, depots and manufactures, often assembling locomotives to the designs of other companies. All these, along with the various designs, became the responsibility of the GWR on takeover, and followed its standardisation of components where this was possible. These works became the beating heart of the GWR's vast empire, where majestic engines were built and maintained by some of the most skillful and inventive engineers of the day. Retired GWR railwayman Ken Gibbs presents a comprehensive portrait of the works from Brunel to the final days of steam in the mid-twentieth century, and beyond to the rediscovery and renovation of many of the workshops for their unique heritage.

Visit our website and discover thousands of other History Press books.

www.thehistorypress.co.uk

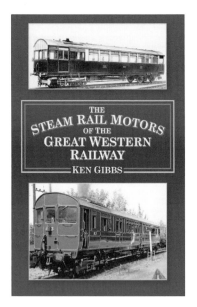

The Steam Rail Motors of the Great Western Railway

KEN GIBBS

978 0 7509 6103 5

Self-propelled carriages were a major innovation at the beginning of the twentieth century, and the GWR was quick to develop a large number of steam motor cars to link farms and scattered villages across the South West to the new branch lines. Their steam motor cars ran from 1903 to 1935, stopping during the war, and were so effective at making rural areas accessible they became victims of their own success. Wagons brought in to meet the high demand proved too heavy for the carriages and they struggled on hills. Soon the steam rail motor services were in decline. After its cancellation all ninety-nine steam carriages were eventually scrapped. Engineer Ken Gibbs reveals the unique GWR carriages, a window into early twentieth-century transport, and the modern replica he helped build, now the only way of viewing these charming historical vehicles.

Visit our website and discover thousands of other History Press books.

www.thehistorypress.co.uk